When in Mexico,
DO AS THE
MEXICANS DO

The Clued-In Guide to Mexican Life, Language, and Culture

Herb Kernecker

McGraw·Hill

New York   Chicago   San Francisco   Lisbon   London   Madrid   Mexico City
Milan   New Delhi   San Juan   Seoul   Singapore   Sydney   Toronto

The McGraw·Hill Companies

Library of Congress Cataloging-in-Publication Data

Kernecker, Herb.
    When in Mexico, do as the Mexicans do : the clued-in guide to Mexican life,
language, and culture / Herb Kernecker.
        p.   cm.
    Includes index.
    ISBN 0-8442-2783-8
        1. Mexico—Handbooks, manuals, etc.   2. Mexico—Social life and customs—
21st century—Handbooks, manuals, etc.   3. Visitors, Foreign—Mexico—Life skills
guides.   4. Americans—Mexico—Life skills guides.   I. Titles.

F1209.K43   2005
972—dc22   2005041584

1 2 3 4 5 6 7 8 9 0   LBM/LBM   0 9 8 7 6 5

ISBN 0-8442-2783-8

Interior design by Jennifer Locke
Illustrations by Fred Dolven

Other titles in this series
Ross Steele: *When in France, Do as the French Do*
Hyde Flippo: *When in Germany, Do as the Germans Do*

McGraw-Hill books are available at special quantity discounts to use as premiums and
sales promotions, or for use in corporate training programs. For more information, please
write to the Director of Special Sales, Professional Publishing, McGraw-Hill, Two Penn
Plaza, New York, NY 10121-2298. Or contact your local bookstore.

This book is printed on acid-free paper.

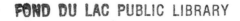

CONTENTS

When in Mexico, do you know how to adapt by doing as the Mexicans do? How aware are you of Mexican customs and traditions? How well do you know Mexican history, contemporary daily life, and the typical domestic routines of the Mexican people?

The following quiz will test your knowledge. There are 111 questions in all, each corresponding to a specific section in the book.

Artesanías

1. Which of these Mexican crafts would you buy to keep warm? ➤1
   (a) *huacal*   (b) *sahumarios*   (c) serapes

2. To which Mexican village should you travel for the best choice of copper products? ➤2
   (a) San Pablito (Puebla)   (b) Santa Clara del Cobre   (c) Metepec (México)
                                (Michoacán)

3. What are typical colors of the Puebla-made Talavera majolica pottery? ➤3
   (a) rustic red and brown   (b) cobalt blue and white   (c) yellow and olive
                                                              green

4. What was the original form of the piñata? ➤4
   (a) large clay jar   (b) cow stomach   (c) stitched tunic

El Norte

5. What are organizers of illegal immigration into the United States called? ➤5
   (a) road runners   (b) coyotes   (c) rattlesnakes

6. How long is the Rio Grande? ➤6
   (a) 1,250 miles   (b) 1,750 miles   (c) 2,150 miles

7. What type of music is associated with TexMex culture? ➤7
   (a) Mariachi   (b) *Conjunto jarocho*   (c) *la música tejana*

8. What proportion of Spanish speakers in the United States are of Mexican origin? ➤8
   (a) one-half   (b) two-thirds   (c) three-fourths

9. Which of the following did *not* originate in Mexican-American culture? ➤10
   (a) zoot-suits   (b) low riders   (c) drive-in restaurants

10. *Menudo*, a Mexican cure for hangovers, consists of what? ➤11
    (a) tequila and beer   (b) stew of innards   (c) lime marmalade

TEST YOURSELF QUIZLINKS

11. Which state was never part of a Mexican territory? ➤13
    (a) Nevada   (b) Utah   (c) Oklahoma

Consumerism

12. What percentage of Mexicans live in the country? ➤14
    (a) 33 percent   (b) 40 percent   (c) 55 percent

13. Place these cities in order of size, from smallest to largest. ➤16
    (a) Tijuana (Baja California) (b) Monterrey (Nuevo León) (c) Puebla (Puebla)

14. What is *not* an acceptable way of shopping in an open-air market? ➤17
    (a) touch the merchandise   (b) haggle over the price   (c) ask to sample wares
        before buying   of groceries

15. At what time should you arrive when invited to a Mexican's home? ➤19
    (a) arrive 10 minutes early (b) arrive on time   (c) arrive one hour late

16. What will you find in La Zona Rosa in Mexico City? ➤21
    (a) boutiques   (b) red-light district (c) butcher shops

17. In Mexico there is one car for every how many inhabitants? ➤23
    (a) five   (b) twelve   (c) nineteen

18. What can you buy at an *ebanistería*? ➤25
    (a) office supplies   (b) ceramics   (c) woodwork

Economy

19. How many Mexican live at or below the poverty line? ➤26
    (a) 30 million   (b) 45 million   (c) 60 million

20. What is unusual about the new 20-peso bill? ➤27
    (a) it is embossed   (b) it is metallic   (c) it is plastic

21. When was the NAFTA trade agreement signed? ➤29
    (a) 1986   (b) 1994   (c) 2000

22. What of these is a key component of business protocol in Mexico? ➤31
    (a) punctuality   (b) formality   (c) casual dress code

23. What is Mexico's largest source of revenue? ➤32
    (a) tourism   (b) mining   (c) oil

Education

24. How many students study at UNAM (La Universidad Autónoma de México)? ➤33
    (a) 150,000   (b) 250,000   (c) 350,000

25. What percentage of first graders in Mexico make it all the way through high school? ➤34
    (a) 14 percent   (b) 21 percent   (c) 28 percent

26. Which of these attributes is typically fostered in Mexican schoolchildren? ➤36
    (a) initiative   (b) creativity   (c) memorization

Fiestas

27. What is the Aztec symbol of death, ever present in Day of the Dead celebrations? ➤37
    (a) phoenix   (b) marigold   (c) maguey

28. *Galleros* are aficionados of what "sport"? ➤39
    (a) cockfighting   (b) bullfighting   (c) bear baiting

29. How many days before Christmas does the *santos peregrinos* (holy pilgrims) procession occur? ➤40
    (a) seven   (b) nine   (c) twelve

30. When does the president make his public delaration "¡Viva Mexico!" on Independence Day? ➤41
    (a) 12 midnight   (b) 6 A.M.   (c) 6 P.M.

31. At what age do many Mexican girls celebrate their rite of passage to womanhood? ➤42
    (a) 14   (b) 15   (c)18

32. How does the town of San Luis Potosí celebrate Good Friday? ➤43
    (a) passion play   (b) procession of flagellants (c) silent procession

33. In what city does the president celebrate Cinco de Mayo? ➤44
    (a) Puebla   (b) Guadalajara   (c) Tijuana

Fine Arts and Music

34. What was the famous Aztec philosopher poet Nezahualcóyotl? ➤45
    (a) a king   (b) a warrior   (c) a priest

TEST YOURSELF QUIZLINKS

35. Which Mexican author wrote *Como agua para chocolate?* ➤48
    (a) Elena Poniatowksa   (b) Octavio Paz   (c) Laura Esquivel

36. Which is the smallest guitar played in a mariachi band? ➤49
    (a) *la guitarra*   (b) *el guitarron*   (c) *la vihuela*

37. For what art style is José Clemente Orozco famous? ➤50
    (a) *muralismo*   (b) dadaism   (c) postmodernism

38. Frida Kahlo was imprisoned in connection with what? ➤52
    (a) antigovernment protest   (b) Trotsky's assassination   (c) obscene paintings

39. What type of Mexican music commonly celebrates current heroes? ➤54
    (a) *corrido*   (b) bolero   (c) *la música ranchera*

40. Which children's movie was directed by Mexican Alfonso Cuarón? ➤55
    (a) *A Series of Unfortunate Events*   (b) *Harry Potter and the Prisoner of Azkaban*   (c) *The Invincibles*

41. What dance is also known as the Mexican Hat Dance? ➤57
    (a) *La macarena*   (b) *La bomba*   (c) *El jarabe tapatio*

Folklore

42. The bark of which of these trees is *not* used to make *papel amate* (Aztec paper)? ➤58
    (a) ash   (b) mulberry   (c) wild fig

43. The costume of a foreign princess who was naturalized in the late 1600s is a treasured exhibit at the Puebla State Museum. From what country did she come? ➤59
    (a) Thailand   (b) China   (c) Russia

44. What ethnic group provides most of the *voladores* (flying men)? ➤60
    (a) Totonac Indians   (b) Huichol Indians   (c) Tarasca Indians

45. What is La Llorona, a frightening figure of Mexican folklore? ➤61
    (a) female werewolf   (b) weeping woman   (c) Aztec princess

46. According to Mexican superstition, what day should you *not* get married on or go on a trip? ➤62
    (a) Tuesday   (b) Wednesday   (c) Thursday

Food

47. How much corn do Mexicans eat per person per year? ➤63
    (a) 200 pounds   (b) 300 pounds   (c) 400 pounds

48. What food item is a small thick patty with beans and salsa spread over the top? ➤64
    (a) *chalupa*   (b) *gordita*   (c) *chaquile*

49. How much maguey core is required to make one quart of tequila? ➤65
    (a) 8 pounds   (b) 10 pounds   (c) 15 pounds

50. Which of the following is a culinary specialty of Oaxaca? ➤66
    (a) beetles   (b) grasshoppers   (c) scorpions

51. When do Mexicans typically have dinner? ➤67
    (a) 6 P.M.   (b) 8 P.M.   (c) 10 P.M.

52. Put these peppers in order of increasing "hotness." ➤68
    (a) chipotle   (b) jalapeño   (c) tabasco

53. What region is known for the culinary specialty of *sopa de caguama* (turtle stew)? ➤69
    (a) Guerrero   (b) Yucatán   (c) Baja California

Government

54. Who was the first Mexican president from the PRI party? ➤70
    (a) Zedillo Ponce de León   (b) Vicente Fox   (c) Lázaro Cárdencas

55. How long can the president of Mexico remain in office? ➤71
    (a) one 6-year term   (b) two 5-year terms   (c) unlimited 4-year terms

56. What is the 9/11 attack on the World Trade Center called in Mexico? ➤73
    (a) *miercoles negro*   (b) *el once negro*   (c) *el nueve once*

History

57. Named for the historical figure La Malinche, what is *malinchismo*? ➤74
    (a) charity   (b) treachery   (c) female assertiveness

58. What was Cortés' occupation when he first came to the Americas? ➤75
    (a) soldier   (b) quartermaster   (c) scribe

59. When did the Aztecs first arrive in the Valley of Mexico? ➤76
    (a) 350 B.C.   (b) A.D. 774   (c) A.D. 1325

TEST YOURSELF QUIZLINKS

60. The Spanish Empire was largely financed by Mexican deposits of what? ►77
    (a) gold   (b) silver   (c) gemstones

61. What was the drink of the Mayan high priests? ►78
    (a) tequila   (b) chile tea   (c) hot chocolate

62. According to Aztec legend, the revered Quetzalcoatl is a feathered what? ►79
    (a) llama   (b) snake   (c) beetle

63. Which of these figures ruled Mexico longest? ►80
    (a) Santa Anna   (b) Benito Juárez   (c) Porfirio Díaz

Home and Family

64. What is the typical role of a compadre? ►82
    (a) financial benefactor   (b) brother   (c) godfather or guardian

65. Who lives in *una casa chica*? ►84
    (a) a child's doll   (b) a husband's mistress   (c) the maid

66. What is the rate of divorce in Mexico? ►87
    (a) under 5 percent   (b) 5–10 percent   (c) 10–20 percent

67. What will teenage boys do when a group of girls start circling a town square? ►88
    (a) follow twenty paces   (b) go twice in counter-   (c) block their way
    behind   clockwise direction

68. Which museum is housed in Chapultepec Park, Mexico City? ►89
    (a) National Museum   (b) National Museum   (c) Franz Mayer
    of History   of Anthropology   Museum

The Land

69. Which volcano in Mexico is closed to climbers because of imminent risk of eruption? ►90
    (a) Popocatépetl   (b) Iztaccíhuatl   (c) Citlaltepetl

70. Which of these towns is on the "Mexican Riviera"? ►92
    (a) Tijuána   (b) Cancún   (c) Puerto Vallarta

71. What is the population of Mexico? ►94
    (a) 100 million   (b) 110 million   (c) 120 million

72. When is the dry season in Mexico? ►95
    (a) October–May   (b) March–July   (c) June–November

73. What is the origin of the middle name of a married woman in Mexico (e.g., the "Sánchez" of María Sánchez de Paredes)? ►96
    (a) her mother   (b) her father   (c) her father-in-law

74. How many paved airports are there in Mexico? ►97
    (a) 230   (b) 450   (c) 570

Language

75. Which language is spoken by Aztec Indians? ►98
    (a) Tzotzil   (b) Mixtec   (c) Nahuatl

76. Which of the following is *not* a "Spanglish" term? ►99
    (a) *jonron* (home run)   (b) *chequear* (to check)   (c) *haquero* (computer hacker)

77. Which of these words in English did *not* originate from the Spanish? ►100
    (a) chaparral   (b) saddle   (c) lasso

78. How do Mexicans pronounce the name of their country? ►101
    (a) me-h-ico   (b) me-sh-ico   (c) me-ksi-co

79. According to the Mexican saying, "One bird in the hand is worth" what? ►103
    (a) two in the tree   (b) ten in the field (c) one hundred flying

80. According to the American Council on the Teaching of Foreign Languages, learners need how many years of language study to be "generally understood" by sympathetic native speakers? ►105
    (a) one year   (b) two years   (c) four years

81. What is the common form of greeting between acquaintances in Mexico? ►107
    (a) handshake only   (b) handshake, hug, and shoulder patting   (c) hug and two kisses on cheek

Media

82. What reading material has Mexico City offered in its subway stations? ►109
    (a) health and safety leaflets   (b) government-controlled newspapers   (c) classics of world literature

83. Which Mexican TV channel is owned by NBC? ►112
    (a) Telemundo   (b) Univision   (c) TVAzteca

TEST YOURSELF QUIZLINKS

84. How many telephone lines are there in Mexico? ►113
    (a) 16 million   (b) 32 million   (c) 40 million

National Icons

85. What does green stand for on the Mexican flag? ►114
    (a) land   (b) independence   (c) Aztec nation

86. When were three hundred protesters killed in a massacre in La Plaza de Las Tres Culturas? ►116
    (a) 1952   (b) 1968   (c) 1974

87. Against which enemy did six heroic Mexican cadets die? ►117
    (a) French   (b) Americans   (c) Spanish

88. Which did Benito Juárez *not* do? ►118
    (a) strip the church of   (b) execute French puppet   (c) lose Texas
        its wealth   Maximilian

Religion

89. When is the name day of Our Lady of Guadalupe celebrated? ►119
    (a) March 7   (b) August 21   (c) December 12

90. What percentage of the Mexican population is Catholic? ►120
    (a) 75 percent   (b) 85 percent   (c) 90 percent

91. Which saint is invoked to help find lost items? ►122
    (a) Santa Genoveva   (b) San Antonio   (c) San Julian

Social Issues

92. For what would you consult a *curandero*? ►123
    (a) legal advice   (b) healing   (c) job placement

93. What are the racial origins of the *criollos*? ►125
    (a) Caribbean islands   (b) Central America   (c) Spain

94. Who are the recipients of *piropos*? ►127
    (a) women   (b) children   (c) street beggars

95. What is your social standing if you shop at *tianguis*? ►128
    (a) affluent   (b) middle class   (c) poverty line

96. How much of the Mexican population is under age fifteen? ➤130
    (a) one-quarter   (b) one-third   (c) two-fifths

97. What would you get at CONASUPO? ➤132
    (a) subsidized food   (b) family planning advice   (c) tax refunds

Sports and Entertainment

98. Who makes the draw, broadcast on TV, for the National Lottery? ➤134
    (a) president of the   (b) twelve schoolchildren   (c) different celebrity
    National Lottery   each week

99. What was the Aztec game of tlachtli played with? ➤133
    (a) human skull   (b) rubber ball   (c) avocado stone

100. What will you see at a *charreada*? ➤136
    (a) rodeo   (b) drag races   (c) Mexican NASCAR
                                                          races

101. When was soccer introduced into Mexico? ➤137
    (a) 1880   (b) 1900   (c) 1920

102. When was the first bullfight held in Mexico? ➤138
    (a) eleventh century A.D.   (b) 1529   (c) 1787

103. What distinctive clothing do most Mexican wrestlers wear? ➤139
    (a) a mask   (b) shoulder pads   (c) short-legged boots

Tourism

104. Where will you find *topes*? ➤140
    (a) middle of the road   (b) side of the road   (c) above the road

105. On which travel route does the city of Palenque lie? ➤141
    (a) La Ruta de Las Flores (b) El Camino Real   (c) La Ruta Maya

106. Where do the *chilangos* live? ➤142
    (a) Mexico City   (b) Yucatán   (c) Acapulco

107. In which city, in the ancient capital of Toltec Empire, can you see 14-foot warrior figures? ➤143
    (a) Tula   (b) Chihuahua   (c) Zacatecas

TEST YOURSELF QUIZLINKS

108. Where would you find the ruins of Monte Albán, the largest tree in the Americas, and *mescal* distilleries? ➤144
    (a) Oaxaca   (b) Tuxtla   (c) Tehuacán

109. Which of these songs is most appropriate to ask a mariachi band to play? ➤145
    (a) "La bamba"   (b) "La vida loca"   (c) "El rey"

110. Which of the following cities is a popular area for American expatriates? ➤147
    (a) Cuidad Juárez   (b) Cuernavaca   (c) Veracruz

111. Which of the following is *not* required when driving a private vehicle into Mexico? ➤148
    (a) credit card   (b) tourist card   (c) international driver's license

When in Mexico, Do as the Mexicans Do is meant to encourage curious travelers to live experiences that depart from their customary environment and to immerse themselves into a culture that geographically is so close, yet spiritually so far away. Cultural immersion in Mexico will guarantee an exciting roller-coaster ride through the heights of participating in unrestrained *celebraciones, fiestas, y ferias,* as well as the downs of commiserating with the daily struggle and abject poverty.

"¡Como México no hay dos! (There are no two Mexicos!)" they may shout in exuberant moments when *la pachanga* (fiesta) is in full swing, but also mumble and sigh the very same words in the next moment when they have come to the end of their rope, all over again. Once the visitor recognizes how seemingly careless and matter-of-factly the Mexicans shrug off hardship and take what comes, it quickly becomes obvious that pity or envy never belong or fit into that environment. "Carpe diem (Seize the day)" is the Mexicans' philosophy of life, *la pura vida.*

The saying "when in Mexico, do as the Mexicans do" is an open invitation to an exciting adventure. It means, for example, strolling along the beaches of Zihuatanejo, squeezing into the overcrowded subway in Mexico City, sipping homegrown coffee on the zocalo of San Cristóbal de las Casas, riding a burro to get to that remote village in Oaxaca, enjoying the indescribably delicious aromas of a bustling marketplace, rolling up a tortilla to use as a utensil for scooping up black beans, spoiling yourself in a fancy restaurant in the Acapulco Princess Hotel, relaxing when the water supply runs out while you stand in the shower—fully soaped, inviting you to a feast in the graveyards on the Day of the Dead, marveling at incredible landscapes, dancing to *la música que toca y toca* (the music that never stops playing), looking with excitement for just the right *artesanía* (piece of popular art) for your living room, and, finally, making you drunk with too much of everything, including life, and, maybe, tequila.

The following glimpses of Mexico, its dazzling colors of life, culture, traditions, problems, and joy, hope to reduce anxiety and rash judgments based on unrealistic comparison with your own set of cultural values. These views of Mexican existence are intended to arouse your interest and curiosity to understand more of the Mexican way of life and help you appreciate more deeply the prevailing kindness of the people to strangers, especially when they recognize your desire to overcome barriers of language and differences in appearance, economic status, and nationality.

And yet it takes foreigners a long time to blend in. They never will quite be indigenous. The mere fact of taking a leisure trip to Mexico and living or working there sets the traveler worlds apart from most of the people he'll encounter. But looking, listening, speaking, and trying to do things as the Mexicans would do them will open many a door to an unforgettable and genuine Mexican experience.

Palenque, Mayan pyramid

Artesanías mexicanas: Mexican Arts and Crafts

Popular arts anywhere genuinely express societal values and the cultural uniqueness of a nation. While all over the industrial Western world mass-produced articles are replacing popular arts, in Mexico thousands of *artesanos* (craftsmen) are carrying on traditions they learned from their forefathers. This reflects not only a deep appreciation for tradition, but also the necessity to create "things Mexican" that are tuned to everyday needs and enable survival during economic hardship. It is still more reasonable to haggle over a handmade clay *olla* in the daily open air market than to buy a stainless steel pot in an urban *supermercado*.

The government agency, El Fondo Nacional de Artesanías (FONART, the national fund for folk art), promotes the survival of regional arts with slogans such as *"El arte popular es patrimonio cultural de Mexico* (Popular art is the heritage of Mexico)." It is, and will continue to be, very successful just as long as local and tourist demands are met, because most products of this ubiquitous cottage industry originally catered to the local market. That way, a *huacal*, a Totonac baby carrier from the Huasteca region, can be repurposed as a handy magazine holder—or an interesting "conversation piece" in a tourist's home.

This exuberant creativity often blurs the already fuzzy line between popular and fine arts. A lifelong repetition of traditional shapes, designs, and patterns deepens the skill of the artisan and enables him to unleash his creative forces.

And there we look at the *alfarero* (potter) who works throughout the year to produce traditional *sahumarios* (incense burners) for *el día de los muertos*, or the makers of *amatl*, the bark paper once sacred to recording the Aztec codices but now brightly painted and displayed in the tourist markets, or tightly woven serapes of natural wool to keep the local as well as the visitor warm, or the many ingenious and colorful toys designed to teach perseverance and entertain at the same time.

For this incredibly wide palette of traditional artistic skills, Mexico relies on an equally varied range of sources: the pre-Columbian component, the cross-fertilizing years of colonization, the still persevering and reliable traditions of regionally distinct ethnic groups, and the steady influence of the predominant mestizo culture that wants to connect to modern society. On the one hand it jealously attempts to guard the national heritage while on the other being unable to escape the ever-present threat of global standardization and mass production.

Related Web link: fonart.gob.mx—Mexican arts and crafts (S)

1

The Popular Arts Route: It Takes a Village

Mexico's endless variety of popular art is well represented in tourist shops all around the country—La Zona Rosa in Mexico City with its arts and crafts from all over the country is a good example. These markets and vendors are also a good resource to actually track down the origin of some of those artifacts—information that can direct an interested tourist to some fascinating itineraries. Throughout the country there are pueblos where many families traditionally have earned a living for generations by creating very specific artifacts based on locally available resources and marketability.

Interested in ceramics? Find an abundant choice of destinations ranging from San Bartolo Coyotepec in Oaxaca for black burnished pottery, to Metepec (México) for *árboles de la vida* (trees of life), to Puebla (Puebla), Dolores Hidalgo (Guanajuato), or the area of Guadalajara for fancy Talavera dishes.

Paracho, a small town in the state of Michoacán, is all about *guitarras*, violins, and cellos. Two-thirds of all Mexican guitars are made here, and the best of them compete well on the international market. Fragrant cedar chests and boxes, lacquered and decorated with intricate designs, come from the remote village of Olinalá (Guerrero). And blankets, serapes, and rugs await in Teotitlán del Valle (Oaxaca), masterfully made according to pre-Hispanic weaving traditions and using a wide variety of design—indigenous, zoomorphic, and modern.

Another well-known artisans' town is Santa Clara del Cobre (Michoacán). Copper products—kettles, pots, plates, candlesticks, and lamps skillfully hammered into shiny works of art—dominate the showrooms and line the streets.

San Pablito, in the north of the state of Puebla, where the art of making bark paper has survived since pre-Columbian times, is more than worth a visit. As you approach the *pueblito* (small village), a constant "toc-toc" tells that the women are busy pounding the bark into sheets of paper. And continuing on the route to Amayaltepec in Guerrero, one can watch skilled painters decorate those sheets with colorful drawings.

One final example for the adventurous: north of the capital of Hidalgo in a remote valley, the village of Tlahuelompa has stayed off the beaten track for centuries. Here, the tradition of bell-making survives from early colonial days.

Talavera jar, Puebla

Related Web link: fonart.gob.mx/catalogo— FONART, government website (S)

Pottery

With the delivery of *un burro de barro*, a donkey-load of clay earth from *el monte* (mountain side, or "out there"), countless family potteries begin the production cycle of their traditional *cerámica* or *loza*. Women and children pound and break the clods and clean off what is not clay. The sifted powder goes into a shallow pit and is mixed with water. When the clay has settled, the women skim the water surface to remove any of the small debris. After a few days, the water has evaporated and the clay has developed a doughlike consistency. Eventually the potters roll up the clay and knead it into manageable chunks, which are wrapped in plastic and stored away.

Mexican *alfareros* then create objects that range from simple low-fired household utensils to sophisticated high-fired majolica ware, reflecting two distinct influences: pre-Columbian and Spanish-Arabic. The colonial period saw limited blending of the two traditions; the Spaniards studied the local potters' shapes and regional designs, while indigenous potters inspected the fascinating potter's wheel and tried out Spanish glazing techniques.

The towns of Tonalá and Tlaquepaque (close to Guadalajara) and Puebla have become well-known production centers that focus on the Hispanic traditions. For example, the Puebla-made Talavera majolica ware, in cobalt blue and opaque tin-white or polychrome, can be directly traced back to Talavera de la Reina, close to Madrid, Spain.

Back in the small family-run *alfarerías* (potteries), the clay is ready. In Amatenango del Valle (Chiapas), women are hand-building enormous pitchers or cooking pots, and, on a whim, maybe a money bank in the shape of an armadillo. In Atzacoaloya (Guerrero), women hand-shape white clay jars and *cazuelas* (bowls). In Atzompa (Oaxaca), potters use *volteadores*, precariously balanced handwheels, to make their perfect jars with raised handles for special occasions. In Tzintzuntzan (Michoacán), white plates are decorated with local motifs, such as fishermen with butterfly nets on Lake Patzcuaro; in Huaquechula, up in the mountains of Puebla, women shape *comales* (clay griddles) that will rest on three *perros* (dog-shaped supports) over the kitchen fire; in Acatlan (Puebla), *árboles de la vida* with all their intricate details "grow" in all sizes and forms; in Salatitlan (Jalisco), it is clay whistles; and around Tlaquepaque clay toy figures are made from molds, to be set up in scenes such as a cockfight, baptism, or mariachi band.

For the firing process, the potters use *leña* (firewood) in simple pits or brick structures. In the factories, state-of-the-art huge gas-fired kilns are common for *cerámica* in the Hispanic tradition.

Finally, the dazzling variety of pottery is either sold on the premises to locals or transported to the nearest market. Some choice pieces will end up in stores maintained by FONART in the capital or tourist resorts, and a few will make it to boutiques in the United States and Europe.

Related Web link: inside-mexico.com/art1.htm— information on Talavera pottery (E)

La piñata

Dale, dale, dale	Hit it, hit it, hit it
no pierdas el tino	don't lose your good aim
porque si lo perdes	because if you lose it
pierdes el camino...	you'll lose the way . . .

This song is indeed music to the ears of Mexican children. It's the piñata-breaking song. It goes with Christmas and the posadas as well as with birthdays and other family celebrations. The piñata has quickly become a household item in the United States, one that is seen at many children's birthday parties, and is often a central feature at events celebrating the Cinco de Mayo.

The custom itself had traveled through various cultures, from China with Marco Polo to Venice and then on to Spain before it blossomed in Mexico. There, this old-world tradition blended readily with a similar Aztec ceremony held in honor of Huitzilopochtli, the god of war, sun, and the nation.

The main idea was to break a suspended vessel containing little treasures, jewelry, candy, or fruit. Because the piñata hangs on a rope that is pulled and swung in unpredictable directions, it takes some time until one of the blindfolded players hits it hard enough to break it. Once that happens, all the good things come down in a shower from above. Spanish missionaries used the piñata as an effective conversion tool: blinded, disoriented, aimless sinners try to break the power of the devil, who keeps back the heavenly rewards. But once Satan's hold is broken, the treasures of heavens pour forth. And the reward is, literally, sweet.

Over the years, the piñata has changed in appearance. Originally it used to be a *cántaro*, a big clay jar readily available from the local potter. After some feathers and paper fringes were attached, it served well for the missionaries' Sunday teachings. In time, however, these basic adornments turned into elaborate shapes and attachments. To appeal to children, zoomorphic piñatas were favored, while star shapes with their seven cones still bear the symbolic message of the deadly sins. From the animal and star shapes it was but a quick step to Disney characters and other contemporary icons. The clay pot changed, of course, to less dangerous materials such as cardboard, papier-mâché, and crepe paper.

Although in rural Mexico decorated clay pots still exist, the supermarket piñata has taken over elsewhere, and children have taken quickly to the lightness of the new materials by continuing their song with:

...esta piñata es de	. . . this piñata is
muchas mañas,	tricky
sólo tiene limones	it only has lime and
y cañas.	sugarcane.
La piñata tiene	The piñata has
caca—	pee—
cacahautes a	peanuts aplenty . . .
montón...	

Related Web link: bry-backmanor.org/holiday fun/pinata.html—how to make a piñata (E)

Coyote, Inc.: Paving the Road to Prosperity

The wily coyote, the jester of the American animal kingdom and indigenous lore, has lent his name to many a foolish enterprise. As a crafty survivor he is often accorded quasi-human status; he is good natured, delightfully irreverent, and able to outsmart the rest of us.

Ahuitzotl, Aztec ruler from 1487 to 1502, chose the coyote for his coat of arms and named places for it (Coyotepec, Coyoacan, and so on); the offspring between an Indian and a mestizo was called "coyote" during Spanish rule; and today the organized "facilitators" in illegal border crossing and human contraband have been labeled *coyotes* or *polleros* (chicken herders).

If the legal migration at Tijuana, both north- and southbound, holds the world record for border crossings, illegal crossings organized by "Coyote, Inc.," in addition to individual attempts, easily multiply these numbers exponentially all along the border from the Pacific to the Gulf of Mexico. Of the 1.5 million illegal immigrants that have been caught since 1996, two-thirds were apprehended by the U.S. border patrol (*la migra*) in the San Diego and El Paso sectors. Points of operation change periodically as *la migra* moves the areas of concentrated activity. At the turn of the millennium, Agua Prieta in Sonora state and Douglas, Ariz., had become the hot spots.

Customers for Coyote, Inc., usually arrive on a bus from *el interior de la república* (central Mexico); they are approached by a *contrabandista*, and a fee, typically between US$1,000 and $2,000, payable on safe arrival in Phoenix, is nego-tiated. After a few days, when the time is right, the actual coyote will guide a small group across the border. There, either a car will immediately whisk the immigrants north or they will wait at a safe house in a town close to the border for the next ride to the north—where payment is due and often made by relatives already established in the United States.

After that Coyote, Inc., lets go. The illegal immigrant, however, is still not safe. Each year, at Phoenix airport alone, about nine thousand are caught and sent back home.

Even though individuals might sometimes get discouraged, the simple law of supply and demand on the U.S. side ensures the flow will continue. Coyote, Inc., having streamlined the business by reducing the violent aspect of the whole operation, may have brought a temporary reprieve to the border area. No more *mojados* (degradingly, often referred to as "wetbacks") swimming across the Rio Grande or the enormous tragedies of undocumented immigrants dying in locked railway cars or under similar mass-transit calamities. Nevertheless, *el camino del diablo*, the devil's road across the southwestern deserts, still takes its grim toll.

Related Web links: bordercounties.org—forum for county governments (E); **cis.org**—Center for Immigration Studies (E)

5

Rio Grande: The Wild North

In the sixteenth and seventeenth centuries, *el norte bárbaro*, the untamed north of the young kingdom of Nueva España, still held a sweet challenge for the adventurous spirit of many an ambitious Spanish soldier and would-be conquistador. The first, officially, to explore that region was Juan de Oñate (ca. 1550–1630), followed by Coronado, Cabeza de Vaca, Escalante, and many others. They did not come to settle and take the land: they were looking for gold of the elusive seven cities of Cíbola, which the earliest explorers believed contained vast treasures.

It was in their wake that priests, tradesmen, and the first farmers and ranchers started settling down. They all endured incredible hardships in their search for souls or a piece of habitable land. They didn't get rich, and the native population all too often resisted conversion to Christianity; open revolution was common, and the land had to be fought for.

The second wave, however, already had some solid reference points, as diverse as the fearsome Sonoran desert and the Shangri-La of the Rio Bravo del Norte valley, the name the Spaniards gave the Rio Grande. Over the next centuries this 1,750-mile (2,800 km) waterway from the Rocky Mountains to the Gulf of Mexico became a reassuring lifeline for the traveling and settling frontiersmen. It was by the banks of the Rio Grande that Oñate and his group celebrated a first American Thanksgiving on April 22, 1598.

Given its geographical isolation this area eventually created its own culture, quite separate from the colonial heartland.

Throughout the following centuries the Rio Grande region became a safe stopover en route to or from the vast unknown. From Santa Fe and Albuquerque at its northern end, the Camino Real (royal road) from Mexico City to the colonial outposts had, by the early 1800s, become the link to most of the European settlements in what is now the United States through the legendary Santa Fe, California, and Gila Trails.

The interaction of the three prevalent cultures—native Americans, Spanish settlers, and early Europeans—eventually created what now constitutes the unique appeal of the Southwest. In its traditions, folklore, and lifestyle it offers a welcome departure from present-day America and attracts tourists from all over the world.

And the Rio Grande? After nurturing vast agricultural development in its valley for four hundred years, frequently occurring periods of drought have reduced it to what could now be called the Arroyo Grande (big creek); it becomes a trickle that often evaporates before it ever reaches the Gulf of Mexico.

Related Web links: nps.gov/rigr/pphtml/facts .html—National Park Service, Rio Grande website (E); nps.gov/bibe/home.htm—National Park Service, Big Bend website (E)

TexMex and Beyond

When the border between Mexico and the United States was settled in its present location, it left thousands of Mexicans north of the Rio Grande under new laws, a new nation, and a new language. They were granted certain negotiated rights but instantly became a unique minority. Their traditions differed considerably from the Anglo/European mainstream culture that established itself swiftly after the 1850s. Although the Mexican population became marginalized, their long knowledge of the land and its resources made an indelible imprint on the border culture, now mostly referred to as "TexMex."

The strongest expression of the TexMex idea is to be found in food. It is where the original *cocina norteña* (northern Mexican frontier foods) were complemented with a variety of other ingredients and adjusted to suit the tastes of many. The dishes concocted on that basis had a strong resemblance to the original Mexican cuisine but were, and still are, adaptations for the broader U.S. palate.

In the early days of cultural isolation Mexicans in Texas cooked beans, rice, and chiles, with meat on special occasions, while German, Czech, and Polish immigrants were working on their sauerkraut supply, smoking meat, and stuffing sausages. Even though all these different ingredients never successfully mingled, the social scene clearly did. At community gatherings and dances, out came *las guitarras* and the Europeans' accordions and a unique new sound was created, *la música tejana*, the second most prominent component of TexMex culture. Today it is still a genre to itself and widely played on either side of the border.

The concept of TexMex is not unique to the area where Texas and Mexico meet. It continues between all the border states — New Mexico, Arizona, and California on the one side, and Tamaulipas, Nuevo León, Coahuila, Chihuahua, Sonora, and Baja California on the other. Few acronyms have emerged besides CalMex, reflecting another early and ongoing meeting place of the two cultures. New Mexico should actually be the most prominent and first U.S. state mentioned, with its Hispanic tradition going back to the seventeenth century. But New Mexicans take great pains not be thrown into the general Latino pool; they proudly defend their Iberian Hispanic origins.

The original TexMex has today become "Any-StateMex." From Alaska to Maine, Illinois to Florida, the Latino/Mexican presence in the workforce and small business has made a noticeable impact on local economies and social institutions. TexMex and its equivalents have spread throughout the United States and even Canada. Spanish-speaking radio and TV stations abound, authentic groceries are widely available, and politicians, as well as big business, make sure to address the potential of the growing Latino minority.

Related Web links: foodtimeline.org/food mexican.html—history notes on TexMex and Mexican food (E); en.wikipedia.org/wiki/Tex-Mex_and_Tejano—TexMex and Tejano music (E)

7

The Hispanic Presence North of the Border

Considering the diverse geographical backgrounds of the Spanish-speaking population in the United States, it is no wonder that any attempt to label this group as a single unit must fail. Identifying random *hispanohablantes* (Spanish speakers) as "Mexican" is, statistically, correct only 67 times out of 100: that person could be Central or South American (14 percent), Puerto Rican (9 percent), Cuban (4 percent), with the rest from Spain, Equatorial Guinea in Africa, or many another country. To complete the picture, there are about forty million *hispanos* living in the United States, which is about 14 percent of the entire population, and makes this the fifth largest Spanish-speaking country in the world.

Once considered a smooth solution, hyphenation won't work with such a diverse group. No one, including the group itself, can agree on a one-term-fits-all approach. Mexicans, Cubans, Puerto Ricans, and Spaniards are geographically clearly defined. Actually so are all others, but their relatively small numbers don't grant them an official label.

The U.S. Bureau of the Census does make an effort to break down the "other Spanish/Hispanic/Latino" group into Panamanian, Colombian, Peruvian, and so on. Usually the people themselves tend to accept the broader terms "Latino" and "Hispanic." Among themselves, however, they clearly distinguish their origins — not in a discriminatory way, but rather on the basis of cultural identity, language, food, and traditions.

Dialects differ considerably between, for example, Mexico and Argentina because of their history, ethnic makeup, and geography. These distinctions rarely present obstacles in everyday interaction. Distancing comes mainly from immigration status and planning for the future. A third-generation Latino, as a U.S. citizen, is firmly rooted in the country. The undocumented worker who supports his family back home in Latin America, and plans on building his future there, hardly gets involved in the society and local events. Every penny is saved and sent home. In 2003 a record-setting US$13.3 billion was sent to Mexico by immigrants in the United States. After oil exports, this represents Mexico's second highest income source. To spread the wealth and to improve the country's infrastructure, officials came up with the *tres por uno* (three for one) idea, where the local, state, and federal governments each chip in US$1 for every $1 received from an immigrant. Since 2000, with this investment, schools have improved, historical sites have been renovated, and health clinics have appeared in rural areas.

Back in the States, the presence of undocumented workers is still very controversial. The argument goes from "we can't do without them" to "they drain our social programs," all combined with heightened concerns for national security.

Canada also seems to attract its share of immigrants from Latin America, but shows only a few of them as undocumented, largely for geographical reasons. The Latino population was nearly six hundred thousand according to the 2001 census and growing. It typically consists of professionals, immigrating with their small families, who quickly blend into the mainstream. They tend to settle in the urban areas of British Columbia, Alberta, Ontario, and Quebec. One was Jorge Peral who, after single-handedly designing all the new peso bills in Mexico, was hired by the Canadian government to work on their dollar bills. And, on the quaint side, a number of Mennonites from Mexico recently emigrated to southern Ontario.

Canada and the United States have always been nations of immigrants and have accepted new citizens according to quotas and qualifications, but Mexico has a quite different approach. It still is difficult to immigrate or establish citizenship. After living there for at least five years on an FM-2 form you can apply for citizenship—

if you're willing to put up with an overwhelming bureaucracy and the many hoops you have to jump through.

While the Mexican government keeps a very close eye on the treatment of their citizens in the United States, it is also fighting to stem the flow of illegal immigrants on their southern border—a line through the jungle that the police guard ruthlessly. Many Central Americans who choose to cross into Mexico hope for better paying jobs there or just want to move on to the U.S. border. In either case, they won't see the *matrícula consular* (an identification card issued to undocumented workers in the United States by the local Mexican consulate), or receive any preferential treatment. They are swiftly deported because Mexico "can do without them" and does not want them to "drain their social system."

Related Web link: migrationinformation.org/USfocus/display.cfm?ID=35—migration, U.S.–Mexico relationship (E)

Borderlands

In the age of hyphenated names the immensely diverse population of Spanish-speaking immigrants is often mislabeled, and all end up being referred to as "Mexican-Americans." "Hispanic-American" seems to be a widely accepted collective name that embraces all the different states of origin, as does "Latino," which makes reference to the Latin base of their common Spanish language.

Originally it was the Spanish Mexicans who carved out their scanty living from the desert environment of the American Southwest, a region characterized by extreme temperatures and hostile interaction with indigenous nations. Survival depended on rigorous adaptation. After all, they lived in the *norte bárbaro* (barbarian north) of a struggling colonial territory, in an extremely isolated situation with only fragile ties to the king and his court in Castile, Spain.

In untiring waves Spanish conquistadors and their descendants conquered, colonized, and tamed what later was to become Texas, New Mexico, Arizona, and California. "New Spaniards" were the first permanent European settlers in what is now the United States.

Today, the Rio Grande, together with fences and steel walls, cuts a neat line (often called the "tortilla curtain") through the land of these first settlers. Take a closer look, however, and this division is not nearly as surgical as it appears on the map. The coexistence of people throughout old and recent history has created many intricate ties. It has influenced languages, cuisine, music, and customs on either side. The border has become its own, culturally distinct area—a wide, uneven belt of about fifty to a hundred-plus miles on each side of the border, where either one of the two cultural traditions is, if not always accepted, at least expected, and lived with. These borderlands have been an ongoing inspiration for filmmakers, writers, and the *corrido*, a musical genre of sung ballads dealing with current events (see page 54).

It is on leaving this bicultural realm that alienation can occur. Americans cross to the south usually for economic motives, a move that is much easier than for Mexicans going to *el norte*. Cultural adaptation is necessary in either direction, but with one big caveat: it's easier to live in the south on dollars earned in the north.

Notably, in social terms neither migrant group in its new environment will be able to reach far beyond the barrio (neighborhood), represented by a protected (gated) retirement community in Mexico, or an overcrowded apartment in California.

The concept of "crossing over" to another culture can be frowned on because it means abandoning old values and traditions for new ones. Given these restraints, first- and second-generation immigrants are generally unable to subscribe to the new linguistic and cultural environment, and often are compelled to create their own world. Throughout the last century this brought about zoot-suiters, low riders, *cholos*, Chicanos, and, unfortunately, gangs, in the struggle to bridge the gap between the two cultures.

Generations in the United States

Five million Hispanic-Americans live and work undocumented in the United States; about 60 percent of them come from Mexico. To stem the flow, *la migra* and the border police employ all the manpower and newest technology available. Since 9/11 the 2,000-mile border has become a matter of grave concern for the Department of Homeland Security, and bilateral efforts are under way to get a better grip on illegal crossings.

Still, through hell (*el camino del diablo*) and high water (the Rio Grande), a growing number of undocumented immigrants tries to cross to *el norte*. Human rights organizations have denounced the mistreatment of aliens by U.S. border patrols. It is alleged that between 2000 and 2003 around 1,600 Latin Americans (mostly Mexican citizens) died from dehydration and heat exposure in their effort to reach the north.

The reasons for the willingness to endure this hardship and, on top of all that, to spend up to US$2,000 on the coyotes (see page 5) are obvious, even in the knowledge that most undocumented workers will live a marginal existence in an often hostile environment. In the end all those obstacles and deprivations don't weigh as much as the almost guaranteed opportunity for financial success—even if this is not yet an option for more than half the Mexican workforce, or for Latin-Americans in general.

Once in the United States, finding a job is fairly easy. The first option is often as *jornalero* (day laborer) for the men and *la*

limpieza (housecleaning) for the women. To work for an established business, some documents have to be provided, but as fake driver's licenses and Social Security numbers can easily be obtained, this usually doesn't present an insurmountable obstacle.

Many immigrants have the vague plan to stay for a while, save money, and then return home. In that sense they are not dreaming the American dream of assimilation into the melting pot by learning the language and participating in society. Many immigrants happily live in a barrio where more and more small businesses cater to every nostalgic desire of their patrons. Here is La Panadería Azteca (the Aztec bakery), next to *la carnicería* (a butcher shop) that provides just the right cuts and take-out meals, La Taquería Michoacana (Michoacán taco shop), La Zapatería Puebla (Puebla shoe store), which also sells dresses for *las quinceañeras y bodas* (fifteenth birthday celebrations and weddings), and La Princesa, a store that sells *joyas y discos compactos* (jewelry and CDs). In the parking lot on Sundays, a *mercado sobre ruedas* (farmers' market) puts up stands and *Rosita's cocina* restaurant offers *menudo* (a stew of innards and a cure for hangovers) and *huevos rancheros* (ranch-style eggs) for breakfast.

This first generation raises its children according to traditional family values, whether this second generation was born in Mexico or in the United States. Spanish is the language spoken at home, but the children have to adapt to and survive the

11

demands of English-speaking schools. This throws the second generation quickly into an unsettling spin. Their interaction with either side can become very troubled. Held back from embracing the new culture by their home environment, they react despondently to the "outside" world. At the same time, they lose respect for their family for not being able to join the cultural mainstream because of being old-fashioned, unsophisticated, and victims of their legal status. They are very susceptible to running with their *vatos* (buddies) who feel the same way, and even develop their own slang. Some of these groups vent their anger by tagging, go on to form *bandillas* (gangs), establish a territory, and defend it violently. That is how they hope to have at least some control over their lives.

This second generation is often the lost generation. Few graduate from high school, and still fewer go to college. Most of them will eventually find a job and, with a young family to feed, survive. After the hard lessons they have learned, being bilingual, and lacking the close ties to the old country, they start instilling American values in the third generation. From here on, the only reminder of their Latino heritage might be their names, and more and more distant *familia* abroad. Unfortunately, even as established U.S. citizens, they can still be subject to racial profiling when it comes to law enforcement, employment, or moving into certain neighborhoods. In the long run, however, and in spite of the obstacles, success stories abound.

Related Web links: coloquio.com/famosos—
famous Hispanics (S); **amillionlives.com/collect
_spec5.html**—information about famous
Latinos (E)

La reconquista

Conquest, occupation, colonization, and migration have been a continuous thread in Spanish history and can help explain the fluid nature of cultural interaction across *la frontera*, the border between the United States and Mexico. In 1492, *la reconquista* of the Iberian peninsula was officially over. After more than seven hundred years of Moorish occupation, *los reyes católicos* (catholic kings) took Granada, the last stronghold of the Islamic rulers in southern Spain. By then the two cultures had interacted on so many levels that the ongoing skirmishes and battles, intellectual encounters at the universities, intermarriage, religious conversions, and the routine of coexistence made the separation lines extremely fuzzy.

Although the war was over, a whole social system of warlords and marauding troops—aimless warriors robbed of their cause—was still in place. That was when Ferdinand and Isabel, the catholic rulers, probably in their exuberance in celebrating the reconquest, gave Cristobal Colón (Christopher Columbus) three ships to find the westward route to India. The discovery of the new world offered their restless soldiers a new frontier. In the years that followed, countless shiploads of gung-ho soldiers, reckless adventurers, and shrewd speculators crossed the ocean in hopes of a quick fortune, led by the likes of Nuñez de Balboa, Hernán Cortés, Francisco Pizarro, Cabeza de Vaca, Ponce de León, and Coronado. Within a short time they conquered the Aztec, Maya, and Inca empires and soon most of the Americas were under the Spanish crown.

It was not until the nineteenth century that Spain lost its grip on its colonies, probably accelerated by the successful independence movement in the United States. However, the newly independent Latin American nations fell into economic and political turmoil. Eventually, Mexico lost nearly half its territories that had been so difficult to conquer: present-day California, Arizona, New Mexico, Texas, parts of Nevada, Utah, Colorado, and, at one time, Florida.

These areas have never quite lost their Hispanic character and *ambiente*. The culture has been kept alive by the descendants of the early Spanish and later Mexican settlers, immigrants, and migrant workers. Some of the more assertive, even militant groups of Chicanos are determined in their demand to win back Aztlán, the ancient homeland of their forefathers the Aztecs, which they place somewhere within Arizona or New Mexico. Of course, nobody would seriously think of moving the border back to the old line drawn from the California–Oregon border to the delta of the Mississippi. However, what the 2001 census shows, with its steadily growing numbers of resident Hispanic-Americans and Latino newcomers, is akin to yet another, if only demographic, *reconquista* of exactly those territories lost in the past centuries. And the predictions are that by 2050 Hispanics will make up 25 percent of the total U.S. population.

Related Web link: census.gov/population/www/ socdemo/hispanic/ho02.html—U.S. Hispanic population (E)

13

Living in the Country

Off the main highways, paved or unpaved, there are countless and barely visible trails leading away into the empty countryside. Sometimes there are people patiently waiting for a bus or driving loaded-down burros (donkeys) and men briskly riding along on horseback. Where can these people live, and what are they doing?

Clearly, the *veredas* (trails) starting at the shoulder of the highways are not the trailheads a passerby might want to take; rather, they are the lifelines of the struggling *campesinos* who, with tireless patience, try to squeeze out a living from their *terreno* (plot). In some ways these pathways represent the economic pattern, or better, the survival strategies of about 40 percent of Mexico's population at the beginning of the third millennium.

The main path often leads directly to *la casa* (the house). It is built of what the environment provides and the regional climate dictates. That may be all wood (from branches to cut lumber), adobe bricks made of clay and straw, *tabiques* (fired bricks), or even concrete. Palm leaves, wooden shingles, corrugated sheet metal, thatch — all are used for roofing. The one main room is for cooking during the day and sleeping at night, when *petates* (straw mats) are unrolled, *hamacas* (hammocks) hooked to the walls, or *catres* (cots) unfolded.

From the house an intricate network of farther footpaths outlines the daily chores of the whole family. One leads to a well, creek, or river. There, women usually wash clothes or get the water they carry back in big *cántaros* (clay jugs) balanced on their heads to fill the huge *tinajas* (cisterns) at home. Women also do all the cooking, child care, cleaning, and caring for the smaller animals.

Men follow their path to *la milpa* (corn patch), *las huertas* (orchards), *el pasto* (pasture) where they tend to *el ganado* (the bigger livestock), and *el monte* where they collect *la leña* (firewood).

On Sundays, the whole family in their Sunday best takes the road to the closest village to go to *la iglesia* (church), then probably sell some of their products (fruit, vegetables, eggs, meat, often crafts) at *el mercado* (market), socialize with their neighbors, and, finally, buy their staple foods and some much appreciated treats for the children.

Related Web link: db.uwaterloo.ca/~alopez-o/ politics/landliberty.html—discussion of land and politics in Mexico (E)

Living in the City

Most Mexican cities provide a comfortable life for their citizens. There is usually a small, quiet, and quite invisible middle class (30 percent), made up of small business owners, merchants, teachers, etc.; an even smaller established upper class (15 percent), owners of land, factories, and larger businesses; and the rest, a huge percentage of people in the everyday workforce, which ranges from noncontract clerical jobs to *jornaleros*.

Every day the teeming city life brings the two extremes of Mexican society into immediate contact—shockingly so, without much presence of an essential buffering middle class. Even for the casual traveler and observer, the void between the haves and the have-nots is very evident. The poor and the abject are as visible as the rich and super rich. There seems to be no substantial trickle-down effect from big business and corporations as in other capitalist nations from social benefits and care that could increase a prospering working, as well as clerical, middle class.

Still, in all dense population centers, opportunities for making a few pesos abound. There seem to be endless creative variations of what can be sold or services rendered, and what would elicit a few coins from a passerby. Myriads of street vendors sell it all: from *chicle* (chewing gum) to gaudy Disney lamps, from Yucatán hammocks to little cups of chocolate pudding, from lottery tickets to live iguanas. Others offer their services—windshield washing, car watching, shoe shining, etc., are done before one can actually agree. Then there are the performers: flame throwers, body piercers, Aztec dancers, indigenous musicians, acrobats, a mother with a baby, or a handicapped person simply expecting a handout. Competition, however, is fierce. The sheer numbers of people fighting for the residue of the city's economy can be overwhelming. And, strangely enough, also invigorating. It has the appeal of *la pura vida*, raw life. That kind of survival is not always gracious to watch, but seeing the endless patience and still so many smiling, hopeful faces appreciating the positive, as small as it might be, surprises most visitors. The life of the poor is relentless, day and night, right in front of everybody, on sidewalks, in *zaguanes* (entryways), and on empty lots.

The well-off and super rich swoop by in shiny cars and hang out in the ritzy *colonias* (districts). At night, when they finally retire behind high glass-studded walls that surround their mansions in Las Lomas, San Angel, the poor sleep right in the streets or disappear in some overcrowded apartments and shacks in slums such as Nezahuacóyotl, Mexico's biggest and fastest growing shantytown on the eastern outskirts of Mexico City, on the dry dusty bottom of former Lake Texcoco. There, ongoing migration from the country to the city has created insurmountable problems for the city. How can it provide a functioning infrastructure—water, sewers, garbage collection, electricity, jobs, health services, and police—in areas where growth cannot be checked?

The greater Mexico City area, the whole valley of Anáhuac (now exceeding twenty-one million inhabitants), suffers the **15** most of all. Other large urban areas, such as Monterrey (population 4 million), Guadalajara (5 million), Puebla (2 million), Tijuana (1.5 million), and Veracruz and Acapulco (both 1.5 million), have their own, although less severe, growing pains.

Life in the city has to be reinvented daily. It is based on goodwill, hope, inter- dependency within the hierarchy, and the belief that there is something to gain for everybody. It's a transparent but confusing showcase of opportunities, or many a lonesome struggle in the *Labyrinth of Solitude*, so masterfully constructed by the Mexican philosopher and Nobel laureate, Octavio Paz.

Musician, clay figurine

Related Web link: allaboutmexicocity.com— guide for visiting Mexico City (E)

In the Market

The open-air market, *el mercado*, often referred to as *central de abastos* (supply center), still meets almost every daily demand of the majority of the population. This is where *las amas de casa* (housewives) or their *sirvientas* (servants) get their groceries and household supplies. Small corner stores often provide items forgotten on the morning trip to the market, as do the more modern convenience stores— 7-11-type chains such as Oxxo—or larger stores with complete lines of groceries, from Superrama, Blanco, Astor, and Aurrera, to Wal-Mart in the bigger cities.

But it is *los mercados* that still display the colorful variety of Mexican life and how it used to be. They are an overwhelming feast for all senses. First the smells: in the fresh-produce section it might be the intensive cilantro (Chinese parsley or coriander) or the sweet and delicate aroma of guayaba and other exotic fruit. Fresh baked goods—*bolillos* (rolls), *pan dulce* (sweet rolls)—will first be detected by the nose, as of course will the fish and meat sections. *Talabarterías* or *ferreterías* are permeated by the leathery smell of horse gear. Dried curative herbs and spices are—aromatically—available in a special part where one can also get advice from some *curanderos* (healers) on cures for minor aches, pains, and injuries—as well as *el mal de ojo* (evil eye).

Incredible nuances of every color in the rainbow will dazzle the eyes of the shopper or visitor: mountains of bright *naranjas* (oranges); stalks of deep yellow, red, and purple bananas; bundles of *flor de calabaza* (squash blossoms); bouquets of freshly cut flowers; dark avocados; red and green tomatoes; *tunas y nopales* (prickly pear fruit and leaves), arranged in neat and counted piles that go for fixed prices. Here are handfuls of solid black *jumiles* (stink bugs), there a bucket full of pale albino *ajolotes* (embryonic salamanders). Among the dry goods, subtle earthy colors of seeds prevail—a wide variety of *frijoles* (beans) and *maíz* (corn), sometimes even *semillas de cacao* (cocoa beans), the essential ingredient for chocolate, are sold.

Busy food stalls will not only address the taste buds but tempt the passerby with enticing smells and the delicious arrangements of, for example, freshly made *chiles rellenos* (stuffed chili peppers), *huachinango frito* (fried red snapper), *molcajetes* (stone mortars) brimming with different varieties of *salsas frescas* (fresh salsas), big glass containers of *agua de jamaica* (hibiscus flower drink), stacks of steaming tortillas, and more—and the price of this "fast food" is always right. Unlike in the bigger supermarkets, the experience of touching the merchandise doesn't come until after it is bought—except for whole fish, which expert buyers closely scrutinize and poke for freshness.

Finally, the ears. The lively picture would not be complete without sound. The shrill and constant advertising of *las marchantas* (vendors) are easily heard above *la música ranchera* from the loudspeakers and the constant hum of people's voices doing their shopping or exchanging the latest *chismes* (gossip). Prices in groceries are usually not subject to haggling. Sometimes good deals are generously **17** offered by the vendors themselves when the aisles get empty after the morning rush. Housewives don't have much time to waste as most meals are prepared freshly, and the preparation tends to be time-consuming.

How long these markets will exist is uncertain. In many bigger cities the old market halls, often unhealthy and rat infested, have been torn down or replaced by new and modern malls, shopping centers, or American-type supermarkets. Smaller towns, *municipios*, still have their market days in the plaza to provide the surrounding rural areas with the opportunity to buy and sell. Markets taking place only once a week on Sundays, traditionally called *tianguis*, cater mostly to the indigenous rural population in the remotest regions of the country.

Slowly, this picture might change. Traveling salesmen from the urban centers and migrant workers coming and going to *el norte* (the United States) are bringing new ideas and different economic patterns everywhere.

Related Web links: semda.org/info/pyramid.asp ?ID=27—Mexican food pyramid (E); **walmart mexico.com.mx, tiendasoxxo.com.mx, superama .com.mx**—grocery store websites (S)

Mi casa es su casa

When a Mexican acquaintance (be careful with the word *amigo*: "friend" has a deeper significance) refers to his house he will always call it "your house" (*la casa de Usted*). But it might be a long time before you actually see it in person. Casual friends, colleagues, and business partners do not have people "over" as they do in the United States after a short acquaintance.

Being invited and meeting *la familia* and perhaps sharing a meal is a very special treat. On such occasions the social etiquette seems to be more formal, especially away from the cosmopolitan areas. Handing some flowers or a good bottle of *vino* (which might be hard liquor, not necessarily wine) to *la anfitriona* or *el anfitrión* (hostess or host) and shaking hands with both is a good beginning. *Un abrazo* (hug) is appropriate among well-acquainted men, as is a kiss on the cheek between women or men and women. Arriving an hour after the agreed time is better than being on time.

La cocina is usually off-limits for visitors. It still is the realm of *la señora* and the servant(s). A popular saying goes (rather rudely): "*El hombre en la cocina huele a mierda de gallina* (A man in the kitchen smells of chicken shit)."

The urban Mexican kitchen may look very similar to American kitchens, although propane gas stoves are the norm and, as food is bought fresh every day, does not always include refrigerators or other appliances. But there are certainly other unusual utensils or gadgets: *un molcajete* (a stone grinding bowl with a pestle), *un molinillo* (a turned, sometimes carved hot chocolate

whisk), a tortilla press, *un comal* (a round griddle made of tin, clay, or cast iron to warm up tortillas or burn off the skin of chiles, garlic, or tomatillos), *canastas* or *cestos* (baskets) full of the typical standbys *limones, chiles, jitomates, ajo, y cebolla* (limes, chilies, tomatoes, garlic, and onion) or exotic ingredients and foods like *hoja de maíz o maguey, piloncillo, jícaras, zapotes, y huazontle*, etc. (corn husks, agave leaves, unrefined sugar in solid chunks, gourd utensils, zapote fruit, and a broccoli-like vegetable). Hanging on the wall are *estantes, repisas y cucharreras, y ollas de barro* (different kinds of shelves, spoon holders, and clay cooking bowls). Traditional old kitchens are often tiled with *azulejos*, often colorful Talavera tile from Puebla.

Kitchens in rural and tropical areas are often simpler; with no appliances besides *una licuadora* (a blender) for salsa and juice making, the kitchenware mostly hanging from the wall or ceiling, and *la hoguera* (the fireplace or some form of wood-burning stove) right in the center of the room.

Back at the dinner, some *botanas* (snacks) and *cervezas* (beer) or "cubas" (rum and Coca-Cola) have been served in *la sala* (the living room). Hardly any house has carpeted floors; stone tiles or linoleum are the usual choices. The topics of conversation are general. Talking about family life, sports, and good gossip is always accepted, but politics, religion, and social issues and problems should probably be avoided, depending again on the degree of friendship. At around 10 P.M. dinner might **19**

CONSUMERISM

be ready and served in *el comedor* (dining room). Before starting to eat, the host toasts to the guests and everybody exchanges un *"buen provecho"* (literally, "good benefit" = enjoy your meal). Most likely *una sirvienta* (also frequently called *empleada* or simply *muchacha*) will serve the three or four courses plus coffee. Afterward, en *la sobremesa* (literally, "after table") conversation continues over *un desempanse* (a shot of brandy, tequila, or whiskey), a smoke, and more coffee. Often, men, women, and children form separate groups. In intellectually aspiring families the host might suggest *un discurso de sobremesa*, such as an after-dinner speech, or have everyone recite famous poetry. Favorites are poems by Sor Juana Inés de la Cruz, Pablo Neruda, or Garcia Lorca as well as excerpts from heroic epics. Somebody might even sing a favorite song. People seem to enjoy this kind of entertainment and are usually quite prepared to perform.

Clothes

The wide variety in styles and colors of indigenous clothing brightens up the streets all over Latin America, has tourists delighted and eager for souvenirs, and has survived outside influence and coexisted with the cosmopolitan styles of Caracas, Santiago de Chile, or México D.F. Frida Kahlo's famous painting from 1939, "The Two Fridas," shows that coexistence and familiarity—yet clear distinction—between the Mexican and European styles.

According to what goes in La Zona Rosa in Mexico City, the upper class flocks toward exclusive boutiques, to the more prestigious department stores such as Liverpool, and to new malls with all the brand names and current styles advertised in the global media. Disparity in buying power might divert the majority of the people to the booming new shopping centers with a Wal-Mart, Sam's Club, or Palacio de Hierro, which all offer more affordable brands. A wide selection can be found in the countless stores en el centro (downtown) of any Mexican town, from clothing and accessories to cosmetic products. Some items might be *fayuca* (contraband), but if the price is right, who can resist?

As for traditional indigenous apparel, the concept of fashion fades when the environment and custom dictate what to wear, as used to be the case in the rural areas of Mexico. Then, climate was a major designer along with any other tribal demands. Clothes were, and still are in some areas, made by the women themselves.

En la tierra caliente (in the humid, tropical regions), *manta* (plain white cotton cloth of different strengths) is worked into sturdy pants and shirts for the working men, and skirts and blouses for the women. These blouses turn into masterpieces once they are embroidered with colorful yarn according to intricate age-old patterns that show if the woman wearing it is single, married, or widowed. *Lana* (wool) is woven into skirts, ponchos, and jackets in the chillier highlands—*la tierra fría*.

Traveling along the country roads and visiting Sunday markets in the smaller townships offers the visitor a chance to see the incredible variety of traditional clothes as well as to buy some authentic handmade clothing right from the producer. Tourist stores, especially *tiendas de artesanía*, usually stock a good supply of indigenous clothing, and that would be about the only place to bring together the two (unofficially) most beautiful outfits of authentic apparel: that of a Tehuana woman (native of the Isthmus of Tehuantepec) and that of a Huichol man (native of the western Sierra Madre), who in reality live about one thousand miles apart.

Indumentaria indígena (Indigenous dress)

Women

rebozo	the ever-present long, wide shawl in dark colors, which women often use to carry their babies in
huipil	a square blouse without sleeves
quexquemetl	a capelike blouse
faja	a unisex wide, wraparound sash to hold up skirts or pants

21

CONSUMERISM

enagua	skirt	*chamarra*	a short woolen jacket
huaraches	sandals	*morrales*	square shoulder bags of sisal or maguey fiber
Men		*machete*	long, wide, swordlike knife; the campesino's indispensable companion
serape	blanket (often like a poncho, with a hole for the head)		
jorongo	a smaller blanket, often elegantly draped over a shoulder	*pañuelo*	bandanna, worn tied around neck
tilma	shorter, narrower serape, often worn with a belt	*sombrero*	hat, usually woven of palm leaves

Wheels: Not Always a Car

Many Mexicans have to contend with owning little—and definitely much less than their own four wheels. Many more have to entirely rely on their own feet or those of their *bestias*, the *burro*, *mula* (mule), or *caballo* (horse) in their daily work. But to make a living wheels can, without doubt, make all the difference.

Just one wheel on a sturdy wheelbarrow, *una carretilla*, will start a small business. Loading it up with quick turnover merchandise such as *dulces* (candy), jicamas, fruit, and toys will, at the end of the day, yield a small profit and guarantee at least some daily bread.

Somewhat better, two wheels on a cooler box might increase the odds by allowing the seller to offer cold *refrescos* (sodas), *helados* (ice cream), *raspados y nieves* (slurpies and snow cones), or *cocos locos* (coconut cocktails) along the beaches. Also in this category, bicycles provide an astonishing means for transportation of unlikely cargo and "passengers."

Three-wheelers range from a rickshaw used as a *bicitaxi* to fancy carts connected to the back part of a bike. There it is—a movable stand selling fast food such as *perros calientes* (hot dogs), tacos and other tortilla dishes, *mazorcas* (corn on the cob), or *hamburguesas*. Many of the street vendors just check out one of these setups by the day. *El patrón*, a savvy entrepreneur, often owns a whole fleet. They are stocked up in the morning and, on return at the end of the day, the vendor settles his accounts—and hopes for his reasonable share.

But as to four wheels, owning a car is for most Mexicans still a very elusive, if not an impossible, dream. After all, statistics put twelve people to one private vehicle circulating in Mexico. In comparison, Germany, the United Kingdom, and the United States show one car for every two of their citizens.

Volkswagen started a very successful venture in Mexico that has lived up to its name: "people's car." From the late 1960s to 2003, *el escarabajo*, the original bug, has been rolling off the assembly lines at Volkswagen de México in Puebla and has become the major people mover—as taxi, police car, or the middle-class family pride. Other European and American luxury cars strongly appeal to the upper class, whereas U.S. trucks are the vehicle of choice for farmers and ranchers from Chihuahua to Chiapas.

Because driver's licenses are available only from the age of 18, and considering the economic picture as well as the easy availability of public transportation, owning a vehicle is limited to those who can afford it or have to use it for commercial purposes.

Related Web link: vw.com.mx—Volkswagen website (S)

Shopping

The choices of where to shop in Mexico are overwhelming and still much wider than in many first-world countries. A lack of suburban shopping centers or strip malls has preserved smaller retail to a great extent.

This wide range of shopping opportunities starts with individual street vendors, who physically carry their entire inventory with them. Then come the pushcarts, stands, or bigger mobile setups offering fruit, vegetables, and fast food. This is where the crowds in the street get their "quick fix": salty nuts, a mango on a stick, a cup of *flan*, candy and *chicle, choclos* (hot corn on the cob), a taco, freshly squeezed juice, *un raspado*, and, of course, *perros calientes y hamburguesas.*

The *centro de abastos* (permanent or open-air markets) can include all these. For example, La Merced in Mexico City, reportedly the biggest marketplace in the world, offers all the fresh products at the most affordable prices. Then, everywhere, are *las tienditas* (mom-and-pop/hole-in-the-wall stores), which are usually run by families, not registered, and earning very little. Bigger stores, *las tiendas*, will have to comply with the laws and pay taxes, granting the owners solid business opportunities that put them firmly into the middle class. The merchandise ranges from hardware, musical instruments, *abarrotes* (groceries), clothes, shoes, books, ice cream, medicine, and so on, to coffins. Traditional craftsmen such as carpenters, potters, or weavers often sell their products in a display room up front. Small *talleres* (workshops) and their professional services could also be added to this type of business. They repair small engines, bicycles, and shoes; they weld and make wrought iron in tiny street-front spaces. All these are services a Mexican household depends on and are where *una ama de casa o su empleada* will go as needed on her daily fresh-food rounds. Of course, socializing and catching up on the local gossip is a big part of it too.

Next come the *bodegas* (warehouses) or supermarkets. Wal-Mart has gained a strong foothold in Mexico, with a number of partners such as the Aurrera chain with its subsidiaries of Superama. But competition is strong: the European flagship in the battle for the Mexican market is Carrefour, besides two local companies, Comercial Mexicana with Sumesa and Gigante with Super G. They compete very successfully by constantly upgrading their assortment of the best national and global products. Business is good. Wal-Mart has recently earned its biggest profits worldwide from its stores in Mexico. All these *supermercados* cater to the economically stable middle- and upper-class clientele. They also provide many minimum wage jobs for cashiers and baggers, security and maintenance staff, and short-order cooks. Sorry, no greeters, but there are employees who check in your bags.

Up until now only the larger cities and tourist resorts could attract that kind of store, but change is in the air. Malls, successfully tried out in Mexico City, are now spreading throughout the republic. Just as in the United States, they feature a flagship department store with brand-name outlets around it, from Radio Shack to Victoria's

Secret, food courts with Burger King and Super Tortas (Mexican sandwich roll), and a movie theater. And the concept of "hanging out" in a clean, air-conditioned mall works as well in Mexico as it does in the rest of the world. Unfortunately for traditionalists, that leaves the old gathering places—markets, *zocalos* (town squares), and city centers—deserted.

An upscale shopper might find treasures in many small stores in Taxco, Guadalajara, Puebla, Veracruz, Monterrey, or Acapulco, but Mexico City has a few very exclusive areas that live up to Fifth Avenue or Rodeo Drive. La Zona Rosa—the one and only—eventually had to share with Avenida Presidente Masaryk in the Polanco district or San Angel and Coyoacán in the south of the city. Both can boast a concentrated cluster of boutiques, with something for even the most distinguished taste.

WHAT TO GET WHERE	
librería	books
farmacia	drugs
heladería	ice cream
juguetería	toys
pastelería	cakes
panadería	bread
peluquería	haircuts
ferretería	hardware
papelería	office supplies
zapatería	shoes
talabartería	saddles, leather
hojalatería	plumbing
alfarería	ceramics
ebanistería	woodwork
carpintería	carpenter
florería	flowers
dulcería	candy
taquería	tacos
lavandería	laundromat
tintorería	dry cleaning

La lucha diaria: The Daily Struggle

In the year 2000, with a change in the presidency and a loosening of the PRI's grip on power, hope was flying high among the reported 60 million people in Mexico who barely manage to survive or to get away from the poverty line—hope that the indigenous peoples, who form 30 percent of the population, will be able to participate in Mexico's upward swing, hope that a middle class will be able to reestablish itself after forty years of steadily slipping toward poverty, and hope that economic growth will eventually eliminate corruption.

The popular attitude is still that even with the most uplifting promises of the new government, nothing much will change. To illustrate this ongoing struggle of about two-thirds of the Mexican population, here is a real-life scenario.

Una vecina nahua conocida (a Nahua neighbor) lives in a barrio on the outskirts of a Pacific tourist resort. She is married and has three little children. Her formal education ended after fifth grade because she had to help bring home money. She still speaks Nahuatl, but it is heavily mixed with Spanish. The road to her house is not paved, and there are no lights, water, or sewage lines. She does have electricity, but still washes all the family's clothes down in the arroyo. All drinking water has to be carried home from a central well in the barrio.

During the day she sells *artesanías* to tourists from a rented stall close to the beach. Her family cooperates in making most of the intricately painted and lacquered bowls, plates, and strings of brightly decorated fish. Her husband cuts and trims the basic wooden shapes. She and her children do the rest, which includes painting and applying the lacquer with bare hands to distribute evenly just one coat and skip the expense of brushes. Between them they can average about twenty finished pieces a day, often working while doing the sales.

Assuming that those twenty fish are sold, the whole family would make 240 pesos. With that, new raw materials have to be bought and rent paid for the stall. What's left after one day is about the same as an unskilled worker in the United States makes in one hour. But here, with this sum, everyone has to be fed, every need taken care of.

In industrialized societies a situation like this would most likely bring about high numbers of dropouts, but in Mexico the struggling masses still smile, know how to celebrate, and keep their faith while they work hard. With shoulder-shrugging fatalism the majority of poor people just accepts an often-heard refrain: "*Mientras hay lucha hay vida, y mientras hay vida hay lucha* (While there is struggle there is life, and while there is life there is struggle)."

Related Web link: mexico-child-link.org/mexico -factfile-statistics.htm—statistics on poverty in Mexico (E)

El dinero

Veinte centavos, the big old copper coin of yesterday, has disappeared. It used to be the main trading token in the marketplace, until the established exchange rate of 12.50 MN (*moneda nacional,* national money) per US$1 was abandoned and the rate left to float in the late 1970s. López Portillo, president from 1976 to 1982, presided over this first major and painful devaluation of the peso, which fluctuated excessively over many years until in the 1990s it found its place back at around Mex$10 pesos to US$1.

Inflation and all, the new *veinte* coin of days gone by is now the 20-peso bill. It holds more buying power, of course, than the old copper coin. Nevertheless, it has become the most handled piece of currency in Mexico — some 130 million bills are in constant circulation. And knowing the habits of the population that saves money by stuffing it into the proverbial stocking, the government promoted the creation of a plastic, rather than paper, edition of a 20-peso bill. It looks like the old paper version, but it comes in paper-thin plastic with a clear window that makes it hard to counterfeit. These new bills do cost 50 percent more to produce but hold up about four times as long as paper bills. Further, they stay cleaner, even though the general reaction was that they feel somewhat odd to the touch.

Las monedas (coins) currently in circulation come in eight versions. All now show on one side their numerical value, and each has the well-known eagle stamped on the reverse side. The series includes 10, 20, and 50 centavos and 1, 2,

5, 10, and 20 pesos. The 10- and 20-peso coins have a counterpart in bills of the same value. The six bills come in a variety of colors and depict famous Mexicans. The 10-peso bill shows the legendary Emiliano Zapata (1879–1919), a hero of the Mexican Revolution, fighting for distribution of the land with his famous slogan, *Tierra y libertad* (land and freedom). This bill is still in circulation although it is no longer printed. The 20-peso bill features Benito Juárez (1806–1872), probably the most prominent politician of the nineteenth century. José Maria Morelos y Pavón (1765–1815), a leader of the independence movement after Miguel Hidalgo had been executed by the Spanish Royalists, is portrayed on the 50-peso bill with his trademark bandanna wrapped around his head. The 100-peso bill bears the picture of Nezahualcoyotl (1403–1473), philosopher, poet, and king of Texcoco, now part of Mexico City. A poet and scholar, the nun Sor Juana Inés de la Cruz (1651–1695) graces the 200-peso bill. Called the "tenth muse," Sor Juana is still widely quoted today for her pointed but lyrical criticism of colonial society. Finally, the 500-peso bill commemorates General Ignacio Zaragoza (1829–1862), who, in Puebla on May 5, 1862, became one of the few military leaders in the world to win a battle against Napoleon's supposedly invincible army. Every Cinco de Mayo Mexicans, wherever they are, proudly remember that glorious day.

Beyond 500 pesos (currently around US$46) there were no Mexican peso bills of higher value in circulation. If necessary, **27**

U.S. dollar bills beyond that amount were used. Besides, for everyday transactions in the streets, markets, *tiendas*, and offices, bills of Mex$50 or more were already hard to pay with because of the constant lack of change.

Nevertheless, in November of 2004, crisp new Mex$1,000 bills were issued. They proudly display another (probably *the*) Mexican hero: Miguel Hidalgo y Costilla (1753–1811), *padre de la patria* (father of the fatherland), as painted by Joaquin Ramirez in 1865.

The public reaction is somewhat mixed because people are afraid that this new bill does not necessarily mean increasing prosperity but rather growing inflation rates.

Related Web link: banxico.org.mx—pictures of Mexican money, as well as numismatic information (S)

dolvan 2001

Souvenirs, Zihuatanejo

NAFTA/Maquiladoras

The idea for the North American Free Trade Agreement (NAFTA) among Canada, Mexico, and the United States had been around since the 1980s. The hope was that creating a common marketplace by abandoning import/export duties would lead to better jobs, thus diminishing illegal immigration, raising the standard of living in all three countries, and, especially, boosting the economies of Mexico and Canada. When it finally passed in all three countries it was received with a certain skepticism. The labor unions in both Canada and the United States pointed out that the outsourcing of manufacturing jobs to Mexico would cause mass layoffs and a huge trade deficit. Mexicans who worked for far less would still be left with low salaries. Environmental groups pointed out that by moving to Mexico, the big companies would avoid the stricter U.S. environmental protection laws, small business in Mexico would not be able to compete with the industrial giants' investment power, and so on.

Now, more than a decade after NAFTA came into existence, the discussion continues in the United States. Yes, jobs were lost—almost nine hundred thousand in small businesses, manufacturing, and on family farms. Not all the unemployed were able to go back to school and get better jobs, as the U.S. government had so optimistically predicted. Many people had to move into the lower-paying service sector, particularly those who lacked either the wherewithal to relocate or enough spare time to train for a better job. Others succeeded in actually improving their situa-tion, and positive statistics show that two hundred thousand more jobs were created than were initially lost. Illegal immigration has grown, in spite of increased border security, and so has the trade deficit. Lastly, the free flow of goods and services has ben-efited both countries.

Canada has always been a natural ally to the United States, but NAFTA definitely brought Canada closer to Mexico. Trade between the two countries has increased, and increasing numbers of Canadian com-panies have invested in the Mexican mar-ket. Besides, Mexican professionals can now legally find good jobs in Canada.

For Mexico, NAFTA had one huge positive impact that far outweighs all draw-backs: *transparencia*—(transparency), which allows the citizens to understand the power structure better, see its abuse and corrup-tion, and, therefore, be more empowered in the political process. Opening the borders to investment and international business also meant opening the books to create a healthy base for business deals. This was very painful for the Partido Revolucionario Institucional (the PRI), the party that from 1929 to 2000 had not allowed any opposition, always rigged elections, had total control of the mass media, and had kept 75 percent of the country in economic limbo.

The first six years of NAFTA (1994–2000), with its increasing freedom of press, had such an eye-opening impact on the Mexican population that at the first oppor-tunity of a fair election they rejected the PRI candidate, and Vicente Fox won the presidency for the next six years in a land-slide. Coming from the Partido Accion **29**

Nacional (the PAN), a party that stands on the political far right, Fox, a Harvard graduate, also favors big business, but right away he sent the clear message that things were going to change for the better for more Mexicans. The initial euphoria of having shaken off the Parásito Reaccionario Institucionado (Instituted Reactionary Parasite, or "PRInosaur") soon changed into disappointment that *all* the problems didn't disappear right away. In reality, the situation has improved noticeably. Corruption and crime have been tackled as never before, and the introduction of transparency into politics and reporting has promoted efficiency in public offices and the infrastructure and, above all, an awareness that things can change for the better.

In fact, it has been very beneficial for all three countries to engage in such international interaction, although problems remain. For example, contrary to NAFTA regulations, Mexican trucks are still not allowed to come farther than twenty miles into the United States: Mexican trucks won't pass the U.S. emissions and safety standards as long as U.S. truckers' union lobbies are against relaxing the rules as suggested by the current administration. Similarly, drug imports from Canada are not allowed to flow freely because of protectionism. Such restrictions inhibit many other products and services.

A looming cloud on the horizon for Mexico has been the rapid rise of the economies of other countries, particularly China. Production in the maquiladoras had experienced steady growth in revenue until October 2000, when there was an abrupt decline. The maquiladoras could not compete with the still lower wages in the Far East; their working conditions may have been dismal, but all along a positive outlook had been carefully nurtured. The workers would be able to raise their living standards by holding a secure job with health-care coverage, eventually get more education and training, increase their benefits, move out of the company-provided housing, and slowly make Mexico a more prosperous country of many opportunities.

But reality shows that maquiladoras are little more than tightly controlled sweatshops. The daily pay of about US$4 affords the workers, mostly young women, little luxury. Some companies hand out food bonuses at the end of the week. Additionally, the proximity to the border makes life very expensive and dangerous. Drugs are rampant and, around Ciudad Juárez, a ten-year crime wave of kidnappings and murders of more than three hundred women, many of them young mestiza workers, remains unsolved.

This, and the shift to other countries, has closed some of the border plants that until recently accounted for nearly half of all exports to the United States.

Related Web links: questia.com/popular Searches/nafta.jsp; mac.doc.gov/nafta/nafta text.html; mac.doc.gov/nafta/maquiladoras .html—websites on NAFTA (E)

Doing Business in Mexico

Since NAFTA was signed, more and more U.S. companies have crossed the border to invest or do business in Mexico. The agreement has shortened red tape considerably. Restrictions for noncitizens have mostly been eliminated: foreigners now can own more than 49 percent of *un negocio* (a business), although they are still excluded from the oil industry and other government monopolies.

Doing business in Mexico as a foreigner requires adapting to a new, and sometimes very different, set of behaviors. Formality and respect are both essential for successful interaction. *La etiqueta* dictates formality. Conservative is the word. Casual clothing is out, except in tropical settings where men's attire is a guayabera (a shirt with vertical pleats) and a woman might change a business suit to a more comfortable cotton outfit. In terms of conversation and discussion, sarcasm or starting meetings with a joke is out: this would diminish dignity and, therefore, respect for the business partner as well the purpose of the negotiation. Also, time has a different "weight" south of the border. Time does not equal money. The less punctual a person, the more important he might be. Punctuality is actually considered petty and overly eager.

When everybody is finally sitting down, pleasantries are exchanged first. Business issues don't take center stage until later. Even then, the approach is light and not at all fierce determination. Titles should always be correct: *Señor* is good; *Licenciado*, *Doctor*, or *Ingeniero* are even better. Then, noncommital discussions can follow, probing the mood and attitudes of the prospective business partners. The first meeting might well end with only vague promises, but a friendly and promising handshake.

Veterans of foreign business call these different cultural traits and tactics the football vs. soccer syndrome. In football, the direct and fastest line to the end zone is considered the best option. It is understood that to score you have to push, shove, or run down the opposing players. In soccer, it's all about avoiding direct physical contact, smartly outdribbling the opponent to circle around him. The final winning score is often agonizingly low or just a tie.

Being in someone's face over a business deal will only bring negative results, and direct confrontation will quickly end any prospective deal. Subtle clues have to be interpreted and dealt with carefully. Rarely will there be an immediate and straightforward "yes" or "no." A "perhaps" will sometimes be the most positive answer.

Of course, things are changing. Moving into the global marketplace with all its ups and downs, the bumpy ride with NAFTA, and the inability to compete with the Asian market, Mexico is ready to adjust to the dictates of international business etiquette.

Related Web links: workabroad.monster.com/ articles/mexiquette—general guidelines on social behavior (E); executiveplanet.com/ business-etiquette/Mexico.html— general guidelines on business etiquette (E)

Mexico's Position in the World

In the last ten years Mexico has gone through significant changes. Thanks partially to its membership in NAFTA it has opened up its economy, has taken a leading role amongst the developing countries, and, according to the World Bank, is now the world's ninth largest economy.

Its number one partner is the United States, with trade worth US$241 billion a year; the European Community stands in second place and Canada third. Other important partners on the Pacific Rim are Japan, Singapore, and Australia. Mexico also plays a prominent role throughout Latin America and has become a well-respected economic and political leader. In the Business Competitiveness Ratings, compiled by the World Economic Forum, it holds 45th place worldwide out of 147 countries.

Mexico's main asset is petroleum—it is the world's sixth largest oil producer. The second is mining, and third, is the money sent back home by migrant workers in the United States. This contributes a huge amount of foreign currency, as does tourism (six million people a year), which boosts employment in the service industry. Only 25 percent of the population works in agriculture, cultivating and exporting coffee, vegetables, cotton, wheat, cocoa beans, corn, soybeans, tomatoes, and much more. About the same number of people work in industry, including the many maquiladoras. The rest of the population works in the service industry, from the balloon vendor in Chapultepec Park to the more securely employed reception clerk at an Acapulco hotel or fireman, policeman, teacher, nurse, doctor, captain of a cruise ship, tourist guide, computer technician, and many more, whose incomes range from poverty level (40 percent of the population) to a decent living as a trained professional in a secure job. The average gross domestic product per capita, translated into purchasing power, is US$9,000 per year (US$37,000 in the United States, US$27,700 in the United Kingdom). *Los de abajo*, the lowest 10 percent in the income group, consume less than 2 percent, while at the opposite end the top 10 percent take 36 percent, not so radically different from the United States (2 percent and 31 percent, respectively).

Mexico is also a major exporter of cultural "merchandise." Mexican music is listened to all over the Americas and Europe. Who has not heard "La bamba," "La cucaracha," or "Cielito lindo"? And who doesn't instantly think *¡fiesta!* with tequila, *cerveza*, and a huge selection of *refrescos* all being very marketable exports. Mexico projects an easygoing, somewhat exotic, and happy image that sells very well to the more pragmatic and serious people of North America.

Finally, there are the Mexican-made *telenovelas*, a huge industry that produces endless series of melodramatic soap operas with promising names like *Prisionera* (The Prisoner), *La heredera* (The Heiress), or *Amarte es mi pecado* (Loving You Is My Sin).

Related Web links: telemundo51.com/prisionera/index.html, tvazteca.com/telenovelas/heredera —Mexican *telenovelas* (S)

Public Education

Although the opportunity may be lacking, every child in Mexico has the right and obligation to go to school. The system in place structures very rigidly the formative years of young citizens into a prescribed sequence of schooling. The three- to five-year-old, according to La Secretaría de Educación pública (SEP, Department of Public Education), should attend preschool and *el kinder* (kindergarten). This seems to work well for the more affluent, but the majority of preschool children stay close to their mothers throughout the day.

From ages six to twelve (first through sixth grade) there is the obligatory *primaria* (elementary school). The number of dropouts at this level goes into the millions. Of those who continue to their obligatory *secundaria* (three years of secondary education), through the 1990s an estimated 17 millions did not—or could not—finish it. Illiteracy lies around six million, which represents about 6 percent of the population. Failure to complete basic and mandatory education (K–9) can usually be blamed on socioeconomic reasons as well as the lack of infrastructure, especially in rural areas.

From tenth to twelfth grade many students may attend a *preparatoria* to obtain a *bachillerato* (high school diploma) or an *escuela técnica* to become a profesional *técnico* (a white-collar worker). A third option, *la escuela de comercio*, teaches business skills.

Mexico can boast the oldest university in the hemisphere: La Universidad Autónoma de México (UNAM) in Mexico City, founded in the 1550s, is still open and free today to more than a quarter million students who hold a diploma from a *preparatoria*. Students are taught by a faculty of about thirty thousand. There are about eighty other provincial and autonomous universities in Guadalajara, Puebla, Veracruz, Nuevo León, and the prestigious Instituto Tecnológico in Monterrey that operate under the auspices of the SEP.

Frequently, politics get in the way of education and intellectuals challenge the corrupt power structure, which often results in paralyzing student strikes or violent clashes—like the infamous student massacre of 1968 in La Plaza de Las Tres Culturas in Tlatelolco, Mexico City.

Related Web link: sep.gob.mx/wb2—general introduction to public education in Mexico (S)

33

EDUCATION
Statistics, Problems, Solutions

Positive changes in standards of education have been slow but steady. A comparison of statistics from 1970 with 1995 (three years after major changes had been introduced by the SEP), shows that quite clearly. The overall illiteracy rate of the population aged fifteen years and older has shrunk from 29 percent to 11 percent, and is even lower today. In 1975, only 4 percent completed high school compared to 17 percent in 1995. The segment of the population without any school experience has been reduced from 32 percent to 11 percent, while university attendance increased from 2 percent to 10 percent. In 1995, 19 percent completed elementary school (17 percent in 1975), 22 percent finished *la secundaria* (6.5 percent in 1975), and 17 percent graduated from *la preparatoria* with *un bachillerato* (4 percent in 1975). The federal funds spent on education grew from Mex$16.6 billion in1995, to Mex$23 billion in 2000. But still, the average amount of education a child receives is 7.6 years of a mandated 9 years. Only 14 percent of first graders will make it all the way through high school. These figures should be considered in the context of another statistic: 56 percent of all children under five suffer from malnutrition and are, therefore, undersized.

Most problematic are the rural areas of the south with their high percentage of indigenous populations, and the lack of facilities and teachers willing to go there. Ambitious government plans to make preschool mandatory by 2006 are still unrealistic for these areas, further hampered as they are by cultural resistance from families.

The government keeps on struggling with these issues. They have made major progress with *telesecundarias* (TV junior high school), where every day one of five students across the nation follows short fifteen-minute prerecorded lessons on six different subjects with half-hour reviews in workbooks, all monitored by in-class aides. These "schools" not only reach many students but also lower the cost per student by about half (from Mex$12,000–6,000). But, unfortunately, national achievement tests show that only 40 percent of the *tele-estudiantes* passed, and that there is still a severe shortage of monitors/teachers as well as textbooks.

Other efforts concentrate on teacher education. To become an elementary/secondary teacher (first through ninth grade) in Mexico, the *bachillerato* is needed, as are four to six years of attendance at *una escuela normal superior*. Teachers in *preparatorias* with *el bachillerato* are required to attend teacher training colleges or universities, also for four to six years. So it is to nobody's surprise that few of the students who graduate as *licenciados en educación primaria/secundaria* or *una licenciatura* for prep school would rush to one-room schoolhouses in some remote village or *municipio*.

For those that do, it is usually on a temporary basis, making the government's plan for helping rural teachers improve their situation very difficult. To this end, the SEP came up with three programs: First, a community preschool program called "Conociendo a Nuestros Hijos (Knowing Our Children)" with training programs for mothers, children, and pre-

Typical rural school, state of Guerrero

school teachers as well. The program covers health, hygiene, nutrition, learning environment for the families, and coordination skills for the teacher. The second program promotes the famous "three Rs" (reading, writing, and arithmetic) and the adaptation of a curriculum relevant to the rural environment, as well as innovation in teaching methods. Along with socioeconomic activities, it aims to involve the community in the educational process. A third program looks at primary school dropouts from fifth to ninth grade and intends to put alternative learning models into place. Pilot programs have already shown a raised awareness of education in the community, an increase in teachers' motivation, pride in their role as problem solvers, and an ability to get a grasp on rural reality.

Given all that, the prospects look good, were it not for one monster that still lurks in dark corners: the PRInosauro, the old institutions from the seventy-one years of PRI government. The PRInosauro in this case is the National Education Workers Union, the largest union in all Latin America, representing 1.3 million Mexican teachers. They became tremendously powerful because the PRI gave them control over educational matters as long as they guaranteed members would vote for the party. President Fox's election has not yet affected this power structure; on the contrary, the union has managed to reduce the teaching load to four hours a day, maintain veto power over curriculum issues, and protect their teachers even in severe cases of nonattendance. In addition, they have created a system of perks, such as selling open teaching positions to the highest bidder or allowing retiring teachers to pick their own successors, thus shutting out a new generation of well-trained and motivated teachers.

Related Web link: sep.gob.mx/wb2—SEP homepage (S)

EDUCATION
Education and Formation

Mexican society likes to call the upbringing of the young *"formación"* (formation) rather than *educación* (education). Although the terms are often used interchangeably, they are not exactly synonyms. Education is narrower; it happens at school and is concerned primarily with academic and civic development. Formation, in a much wider sense, adds the personality, social behaviors, etiquette, self-respect, and, above all, family and community values beyond the classroom.

The public education system strives to overcome the many regional, ethnic, and economic differences of the country. One attempt is by providing free and uniform textbooks, which are geared toward creating social solidarity throughout *la patria* (the fatherland). A branch of the SEP, the National Commission for Free Textbooks, it is decreed, shall "take great care that the publication of the books of which they are in charge aim at the harmonious development of all faculties of learners, to prepare them for a practical life, promote the conscience for human solidarity, direct them toward their civic duties, and, above all, instill patriotic values based on intimate knowledge of the great historical events that have given the foundation to the democratic evolution of our country."

To promote this kind of solidarity across all levels of society, uniforms at school become an obvious example of the fallacy of that vision: some students just put up with it, others have to struggle to buy one, and a small percentage might even have to stay home because they can't afford one—across the board, again, a perfect mirror image of Mexican society. But no matter what, on Monday morning all over the country, students line up in the schoolyard or basketball court according to class levels, in military fashion, as *la escolta* (flag and escort) parades *la bandera* as everybody joins in singing the national anthem.

Once classes start, it is easy to see the prevalent educational strategies: in Mexico the teacher will most likely be the center of attention. Students see the teacher as an authority figure rather than a facilitator. Students are passive. They answer questions or repeat information—often still in chorus and dictation—rather than engage in creative writing, which could improve communicative skills in their native language. Deductive yields to intuitive reasoning. Memorization and lectures take the place of conversation and discussion in interactive problem solving. Tests are seen as measuring assessments rather than as tools to discover individual potential. Building relationships is more important than competition. The three Rs are the main focus in public schools where neither extracurricular activities nor sports are offered.

Related Web link: emexico.gob.mx/wb2/eMex/ eMex_Libros_de_texto_gratuito—textbooks of public schools online (S)

36

¡Qué viva la muerte!: Long live death!

El día de los muertos (Day of the Dead) is probably *the* unique holiday of Mexico today. For one, the theme behind this tradition resists commercial exploitation elsewhere, unlike Christmas, Valentine's Day, or Cinco de Mayo. After all, who in the rest of the world would want to buy a "Happy Day of the Dead" card?

Most of metropolitan Mexico, the border corridor, and the Baja "appendix" have abandoned intricate celebrations, but these still flourish in the rest of the country. The Day of the Dead celebration is actually the most thorough and successful fusion of Christian and indigenous beliefs about life after death. Also, the date chosen was a compromise between the conquerors' and native calendars. November 1 is All Saints' Day and November 2 All Souls' Day, the two days set aside to think of and pray for *los ánimas benditos en el purgatorio* (the blessed souls in purgatory). The Aztecs had set a similar celebration for their dead in the last quarter of our calendar year.

There are many opportunities to partake in the Day of the Dead celebration. A stroll through the markets shows a wide array of appropriate mementos. Symbols of death permeate every aspect of life: little pop-up coffins for children, sugar skulls and *el pan de los muertos* (buns decorated with crossed bones), special black incense burners, paper banners strung across streets, and the ever-present smell and sight of *zempazuchitl*, the small bright yellow marigold and Aztec symbol of death.

In the graveyards you'll find families visiting their deceased relatives. They bring food, often a *guajolote* (turkey) in tasty

mole (chile/chocolate sauce) and drinks. You hear music, live or from radios, and will get most likely an invitation to sit down and join the feast.

The family may even take you to their house to show you an elaborate altar full of *ofrendas*, offerings for the dearly departed. Portraits, their favorite food and drink, and their most prized possessions are laid out among colorful flowers and fabrics. The *difuntos queridos* (dear departed) might just stop by to gain strength for yet another year of their afterlife.

In this context it is appropriate to mention one artist whose work has become inseparable from the celebration of *el día de los muertos*: José Guadalupe Posadas (1852–1913). His engravings and lithographs criticized the political turmoil of his times, especially *el porfiriato* (Porfirio Díaz' dictatorship) and the many other social injustices. By reducing the objects of his art to skeletons and skulls, he not only employed death as the great social equalizer but also tapped into Mexican people's deep-rooted attitudes toward death. Posadas's inspiration came from a long tradition of satire that started during the French intervention in the 1860s and lasted through the Mexican Revolution in the early twentieth century. He was a regular contributor to the satirical magazines *El ahuizote* and *El jicote*, always trying to test the limits set by the severe censorship. His strength was poking fun at everyday political or societal events by using those dehumanized skeletons. His unique lithographs and prints were quickly assimilated into popular imagery. These "living dead" per-

37

Calavera (skull), *día de los muertos*

fectly represented the abstract ideas planted by the celebration of *el día de los muertos*, namely the one of the dead visiting and making merry with their living relatives. His *calaveras* (skull jokes) were printed on broadsheets and accompanied by critical verses roasting contemporary political figures. These prints were sold right next to religious pictures and paraphernalia at ferias all over the country. Today the tradition of making fun of community leaders, politicians, and celebrities continues. Winning *calaveras*, now trimmed down to only the written verses, are published by many newspapers following fierce local, even national competition in *los concursos de las calaveras*.

    Impending presidential elections in Mexico or the United States have traditionally been a high season for *calaveras*:

Por aquí pasa	Here goes the
el mero-mero,	boss man
pensando con toda	thinking with all his
su mente,	sentiment,
que como ya es	that already being
rey de monos	king of apes
tambien puede	he also can be
ser presidente.	president.

Related Web links: mexconnect.com/mex_/ feature/daydeadindex.html (E); mexico.udg.mx/ arte/diademuertos (S)—*el día de los muertos* websites; analitica.com/va/arte/portafolio/ 8789685.asp—prints by José Guadalupe Posadas (S)

Cockfights

Ferias and other local celebrations frequently include *peleas de gallos* (cockfights). Usually on Sunday nights, *los palenques* (pits or arenas) are set up quickly and men from all walks of life gather around a fenced-off arena. Excitement is in the air as these *galleros* (aficionados) discuss the upcoming fights.

Behind the scenes, the owners of the *gallos* are weighing in the birds. The rules allow for only minute differences in weight between the two opponents, most of which come in at around 2.5 kilos. Government authorities overseeing this type of entertainment, including bullfights and rodeos, dictate the framework for the sponsors of the fights—that is, responsibility for orderly procedures according to the regulations and traditions of the "sport."

As the two contestants are brought out, the spectators quickly compare the *gallos* and place their bets. At that point, the fighting cocks are still calmly handled by their handlers/owners. The birds, their wattles and combs trimmed, look very streamlined and elegantly bored.

As the betting bustle continues around the pit, the cock handlers and aides carefully select the appropriate *espuelas* (razor-sharp blades) from their velvet-lined cases and tie them onto the cocks' blunted spurs. These blades or curved picks traditionally measure from one to three *pulgadas* (inches, thumbs).

After the referee has carefully inspected each *gallo* the fight begins. The handlers roust up their fighters by swinging them back and forth and close up to "teasing" birds, which gets them visibly agitated.

They then place the cocks opposite each other about half a meter on either side of the line running across the arena.

Betting stops as the *gallos* attack. A fight might take just a flurry of a moment to half an hour. Strategic coaching seems important. Even with broken bones or gouged-out eyes the *gallos* might fight on. A handler often treats a punctured lung by sucking the blood out through the beak—just to send the bird right back for a last chance to deal the final blow to the opponent. The end often comes quicker than expected.

And while the winners cheer with the lucky gamblers, the other handler picks up the dead loser. And even though he may have lost a *gallo de la primera* (a prime fighter that could be worth up to Mex$5,000), the owner's passion most likely did not die. He soon will be back with another of his carefully nurtured fighters in one of the many *palenques* throughout South America, the Phillipines, or even New Mexico and Louisiana, the two U.S. states where cockfights are still legal.

Related Web link: surf-mexico.com/culture/
cockfights.html—cockfighting in Mexico (E)

Las posadas: ¡Feliz Navidad!

As in the rest of the Christian occident, many of the folk traditions tied to religious events have been pushed into a materialistic (nonspiritual) realm sometimes called *affluenza*. The metropolitan areas—Mexico City, Monterrey, Guadalajara, for instance—subscribe to a great extent to this hustle and bustle of modern life. Smaller barrios within the urban sprawl or the villages haven't changed all that much.

There, at dusk, nine days before Christmas Day, you could run into a procession of villagers following an angel who walks in front of a couple dressed up as Mary and Joseph, or parishioners carrying *retablos* (paintings) or *bultos* (statues) of the holy couple. The procession stops at various houses, and Joseph sings the traditional song asking for lodging:

En nombre	In the name of
del cielo	heaven
os pido posada	I ask you for shelter
ya no puede andar	she can't walk any
	more,
mi esposa amada.	my beloved wife.

At least twice the procession of the *santos peregrinos* (holy pilgrims) will be refused shelter by the landlord. At a third house, however, after some singing, the doors will fly open for the posada of the day. Piñatas for the children and festive food and drink will be ready as the music begins to play.

The basic posada theme, the reenactment of Joseph and Mary searching for a place to stay in the town of Bethlehem, knows many variations throughout the regions of Mexico. But in general, the nine days seem to lighten up the darkness around the solstice with spiritual and worldly happiness that leads up to December 24, the last posada. From there, the procession proceeds to the church, where the statues are returned and everybody joins in celebrating the *misa de gallo* (midnight mass). Afterward, the Christmas feast of *guajolote*, tamales, and *atole* (a corn drink) or *sidra* (bubbly apple juice) awaits. Children open presents from *el niño dios* (Christ child) next to the often elaborate *nacimiento* (nativity scene), and there may even be somewhere a little decorated tree or branch with lights and *luces de Belén* (lights of Bethlehem = sparklers) on them. Christmas Day itself starts late and is rather restful and quiet. After all, Christmas isn't over until *el día de los Reyes Magos* (Day of the Three Kings, or Epiphany) on January 6.

Related Web links: christmas.com/worldview/mx, mexonline.com/christmas.htm—summary of Christmas traditions (E)

¡Viva Mexico! ¡Viva la independencia!

Independence Day celebrates the anniversaries of freedom from *los gachupines* (Spanish-born citizens of the viceroyalty of Nueva España) and from the heavy demands by the Spanish king.

The night of September 15 is the time to go to the Zócalo, the main square in the Distrito Federal, to feel the vigorous heartbeat of the Mexican nation. National pride makes everyone forget for a few hours the problems that plague their country. Excited crowds wait in front of the National Palace for *el presidente* of *la república* to renew Father Hidalgo's legacy by shouting out his famous *grito* (cry): "*¡Viva Mexico! ¡Viva la independencia! ¡Viva Guadalupe!*" And all over Mexico people watch the president on TV or gather in front of the capitols or governors' palaces to cheer on the *gobernadores* (governors of the states), who are delivering the same patriotic performance.

It all started in 1810 in the village of Dolores, now in the state of Guanajuato. The parish priest, Father Miguel Hidalgo, stood in front of his church and aired his discontent with the Spanish crown and the role of the church in the colonies. He immediately ignited the simmering rebellious spirits of his countrymen and got the independence movement going. It took another eleven years, until 1821, to achieve that independence, but Father Hidalgo, unfortunately, never lived to see the fruits of his labor. He was executed by royalists in 1811.

Now back to the Zócalo in any given year on *el día de la independencia*. It truly is a *fiesta de la patria* (patriotic celebra-tion). The national colors—red, white, and green—dominate the scene as does the *escudo nacional* (national coat of arms), which depicts an eagle with a snake in its beak perching on a cactus on an island—a reminder of the Aztecs' claim to the Valley of Mexico.

And when, traditionally, at 12 midnight the president steps out on the balcony of the Palacio del Gobierno on the Zócalo for *el grito* "Long live Mexico! Long live independence! Long live Guadalupe!" some disgruntled voices in the back might still add "and death to the *gachupines*" (Spaniards) to relive the sentiment of that particular night in 1810.

Related Web link: mexgrocer.com/ mexcocina-sep1.html—recipes for Mexican Independence Day (E)

La quinceañera: Princess for a Day

"La mañanitas," the usual birthday song will do just fine for most any birthday. But when a girl turns fifteen, a traditional selection of songs and dances will come up to emphasize this very important day.

"La linda quinceañera" ("The Beautiful Fifteen-Year-Old") is exalted by this song of Los Dandys, which talks about the transition from girl to woman. "De niña a mujer" ("From Girl to Woman"), another song, does the same. "En tu día" ("On Your Day") and "Mi Niña Bonita" ("My Beautiful Child") are tunes that express the feeling of the parents who are about to present their daughter to the benevolence and scrutiny of society. And then come the waltzes: "El Danubio Azul," "Los Cuentos De Los Bosques De Viena," "El Vals del Emperador" ("The Blue Danube," "Tales of the Vienna Woods," "The Emperor's Waltz").

Many girls still go through the celebration of their fifteenth birthday according to the tradition of the *fiesta de quinceañera* (quince = fifteen, años = years). This is by no means just one of many birthday parties. It's a ritual long prepared and well rehearsed. And expensive.

Nowadays the choice to say "yes" or "no" to going through this coming-of-age celebration is often up to the girl, depending on the social status of the family and where within the Hispanic world they live. The tradition is an old one with double roots. Aztec girls usually got married at sixteen or became priestesses. After the conquest and conversion to Catholicism, the choices were similar. Get married after your fifteenth birthday or enter a convent. No matter what, at that birthday the girl

became a woman with all the responsibilities involved.

From the United States to Argentina, *quinceañeras* are a matter of family pride and a celebration of Hispanic tradition. The Catholic Church also carefully nurtures *las quinceañeras* because a major part of the celebration is a lengthy visit to the church. *La agasajada* (the celebrated one) is wearing an (often) pink, flowing dress, sitting in front of the congregation just like in a wedding. Pomp and circumstance could help the church bring back the younger generation.

Quinceañeras often exceed wedding celebrations in their pomp, circumstance—and cost. The parents have to come up with around US$10,000 to cover the festivities. The event dictates formality to a degree that leaves little choice. There is the girl's dress—custom made, of course—the hairdo, makeup, limousine, church ceremony around noon, and the rental of a *sala* (ballroom), musicians and/or a mariachi band, catered food and drink, and memorabilia such as personalized ashtrays, vases, glasses, napkins, and decorations. Guests are usually numerous and a good time is guaranteed for everyone.

The girl can pick her escort, but the first waltz she dances is with her father. He, and the godparents also, have to give speeches that praise the virtues, accomplishments, promising future, and good looks of the young lady.

Related Web link: partypop.com/planning/ Quinceañera—shows the intricacies of the celebration (E)

42

Easter: *La Semana Santa*

Holy Week, between Palm Sunday and Easter Monday, is nearly as important a celebration as Christmas itself. Many Mexicans devoutly observe and participate in the elaborate liturgy and events in the churches and community. The most interesting events might be found in the more remote indigenous villages from Chihuahua to Chiapas, where the early missionaries so successfully taught the new religion through hands-on methods. The original teachings are still alive in various ritualized and sometimes fossilized reenactments.

El Miércoles de Ceniza (Ash Wednesday), marking the beginning of Lent forty days before Easter, actually starts the season with a reminder of human mortality (after *carneval*). During mass on that day, the priest draws a cross on the churchgoers' foreheads, while mumbling "ashes to ashes. . . ." With this, fasting begins. Nowadays *las ayunas* (fasting) might just mean giving up something like sweets, alcohol, or cigarettes. Many may still eliminate or reduce their meat consumption, and others may go on that long-planned diet.

La Semana Santa, Holy Week itself, begins with *el Domingo de Ramos* (Palm Sunday). The congregation gathers for processions and reenactments of Jesus's arrival in Jerusalem. They carry *ramos* (branches of palms), blessed by the priest, or sometimes fresh flowers, first to mass and then home. There they decorate the cross or the altar that has been put up for Holy Week. Monday through Wednesday the believers throng to church for confession and get ready for the celebration of *las Pascuas Floridas*, the actual days of Easter.

On *Jueves Santo* (Holy Thursday) the Last Supper is remembered. Liturgy often includes the washing of feet during evening church services. *El Viernes Santo* (Good Friday) is a somber day. Extreme fasting is the choice for many people. Most radio stations choose to play only classical music. In some cities—Taxco, for instance—hooded *penitentes* (penitents) with crowns of thorns walk through the town flagellating themselves until their backs are raw. San Luis Potosí is known for the *procesión de silencio*, a silent procession to meditate on Christ's death.

Many other parishes have always had a designated hill close to the church as their very own *Monte Calvario (Calvary hill)*, with the fourteen stations of the cross. This is *el viacrucis* (the way of the cross), which the parishioners ascend chanting *el rosario doloroso* (the sorrowful rosary). In some towns, such as Papantla, Ixtapalapa, and Pátzcuaro, carefully chosen amateur actors perform passion plays throughout the week, especially on Good Friday.

El Sábado Santo is also known as *el Sábado Glorioso* because of Christ's resurrection. *El Domingo de Pascuas* (Easter Sunday) continues celebrating that glorious event, first with a high mass followed by family gatherings with the inevitable fiesta. Then children may learn if the Easter Bunny has remembered them, or play with *los cascarones*—confetti-stuffed red eggs that are fun to crack on the heads of friends!

Related Web links: mexonline.com/semana.htm (E), mexico.udg.mx/religion/semsanta (S)— history and celebration of Holy Week

Cinco de Mayo: One Sweet Memory

On Cinco de Mayo (May 5), calendars show the day in red letters (abbreviated as "aniv. bat. Pue.": anniversary of the battle of Puebla), but the historical event behind it does not appear to match the scale of its exuberant celebration outside Mexico, especially in the United States.

It is, in a bittersweet way, about a battle won and a war lost, fought with desperate bravery and determination by General Ignacio Zaragoza's two thousand ragged troops on May 5, 1862. Against all odds, they defeated the French army of Napoleon III in the town of Puebla—and made all six thousand of them run, temporarily delaying the French invasion. The French had come to claim outstanding Mexican debts and provide Napoleon with a solid home base for his expansionist plots in the New World. After May 5, on their hasty retreat to Veracruz, the French invaders were dispersed and involved in numerous deadly skirmishes.

But, soon enough, the French regrouped and succeeded in seizing Mexico City, the center of power. Then, with the help of conservative Mexican allies, Napoleon established Maximilian Ferdinand Joseph, a Hapsburg prince, as the emperor of Mexico. His benevolent reign did not last long. Benito Juárez, the exiled president, returned to central power in 1867 after the French troops had left. He offered Maximilian an honorable way out by relinquishing his imperial powers and returning to Europe. Maximilian refused, and was executed on September 19, 1867, in Querétaro at the age of thirty-five. The spirit and mind of Charlotte (Carlota), his beautiful young Belgian wife, were broken, and she lived in seclusion in a Belgian convent until her death in 1927 at the age of 87.

And still today, in spite of the imperial interlude that many Mexicans romance, Cinco de Mayo is exalted as *epopeya nacional* (national epic) in numerous speeches, parades, and political rallies throughout Mexico. It brings the nation together in an annual rush of patriotism. Puebla, Mexico's third largest city, then organizes a splendid parade remembering this historical accomplishment in grand style under the auspices of the president. Local schools march along with the mounted members of the Asociación Nacional de Charros (National Charro Association), the representative organizations of the various battalions of the original battle, local dignitaries, and brass bands cheering on the spectators with their rousing renditions of the national anthem.

If the celebration in Mexico itself seems to take on a more military tone, in the United States the Cinco de Mayo has become a day that brings together Hispanic immigrants, citizens, and sympathizing friends from other cultural backgrounds. Although most of these parties revolve around Mexican food, drink, and music, they offer a happy occasion for putting Hispanic-American culture and traditions into the limelight and celebrating cultural diversity.

Related Web links: vivacincodemayo.org/ history.htm, angelfire.com/az/CincodeMayo— historical background of Cinco de Mayo (E)

Nezahualcóyotl: A Contemporary Voice from the Past

Surveying the crumbling architectural ruins of cultures long gone gives us an eye into the past, but the written and decipherable words of literature transcend such "digging." Literature clearly highlights the human continuum. It still sings, agonizes, rejoices, resents, and resigns. Writers' voices from the past are still speaking directly and powerfully to us. Too little is preserved of the great culture of the Aztecs in writing. The codices (hieroglyphic picture books) were almost all destroyed by overzealous Catholic clergymen. Only lucky circumstance saved some in dusty museum chambers all over Europe—accessible enough to allow us a glimpse of what once used to be.

One of those voices of Aztec culture who talks powerfully to us is Nezahualcóyotl (1402–1472), king of Texcoco, philosopher, poet, and warrior. Never to know what would befall his people half a century after his death, he recorded this message about life:

I, Nezahualcóyotl, ask this:
Is it true one really lives on earth, only a
 little while here?
Though it be jade it falls apart,
though it be gold it wears away,
though it be Quetzal plumage it is torn
 asunder.
Not forever on earth,
only a little while here.

Who would suspect such a philosophical mind among the bloodthirsty tribes living around the ancient lake of Texcoco? Nezahualcóyotl even seemed to foreshadow the coming of a new Christian deity by writing:

God our lord is invoked everywhere.
Everywhere He is venerated.
It is He who creates things.
He creates himself: God.

Following up on that thought, he had a temple built to honor his new god who could not be "caught" in an image or represented by an idol because He was "everything, everywhere," and beyond.

Nezahualcóyotl even pondered the idea that all men could be equal. Not unlike the proverbial "danse macabre," he said:

Where can we go, where death does not
 exist?
But for this shall I live weeping?
Even princes are born to die. . . .

To follow the footsteps of this extraordinary man, Texcoco, on the northeastern outskirts of Mexico City, is the destination. There, a larger-than-life bronze statue of the poet-king welcomes the visitor. He ruled part of the Valley of Mexico in a triple alliance with the lords of Tenochtitlán and Tlatelolco for forty years. In Texcotzingo, his center of study and research and now a national park, little remains but the outlines of terraced fields and a rubble of rocks where he used to take his ceremonial bath, high above the daily hustle and **45**

FINE ARTS AND MUSIC

Nezahualcóyotl, poet-king of Texcoco

bustle, looking out over the lake toward the volcanoes, contemplating.

And poetry is still alive among the Nahuas (Aztecs), as the following anonymous campesino voice proves. While on an early morning errand looking back across the valley the peasant observes:

Cuando sobre la	When the day
tierra amanece	breaks
la luna muere,	the moon dies.
las estrellas dejan	The stars disappear,
de verse,	
el cielo se ilumina.	the sky lights up.
Allá lejos, al pie	Far over there at the
del cerro,	foot of the mountain,
sale humo de	smoke rises from
mi cabaña,	my hut,
allá está mi	there is my little
amorcito,	love,
mi corazón, mi	my heart, my little
mujercita.	woman.

Everyday life becomes an inspiration and leads, even for a simple man, to deeper thought, not at all so different from the great Nezahualcóyotl:

Madrecita mía,	My dear mother,
cuando yo muera,	when I die
sepúltame junto	bury me next to
al fogón	the hearth
y cuando vayas a	and when you
hacer las tortillas	make tortillas
allí por mí llora.	there you cry for me.
Y si alguien te	And if anybody
preguntara:	asks,
"Señora, ¿por	"Señora, why are
qué lloras?"	you crying?"
dile que está	tell them that the
verde la leña,	firewood is green
hace llorar con	and makes you cry
el humo.	with all the smoke.

Related Web link: mexconnect.com/mex_/ history/jtuck/jtnezahualcoyotl.html— biographical information on Nezahualcóyotl (E)

Mexican Literature

To record preconquest poetry, song, and sacred hymns was initially not on the minds of the conquistadors, and indeed destruction of the blooming indigenous fine arts in all its forms took many forms. Physical looting and burning, as well as mass murder and death from epidemics set off by the Spaniards—all saw many carriers of the oral tradition perish.

Once the dust had settled down, there reappeared the poetry of Nezahualcóyotl, the "Popol Vuh" (the creation story of the Maya), and the books of the Chilam Balam (the jaguar priest), gathering legends, myths, history, beliefs, and the knowledge of the Mayas in the sixteenth century. Then, indigenous *sabios* (learned men) were allowed to continue their cultural traditions and put together *El códice Ramírez, La crónica mexicana,* and *La historia mexicana.*

At the same time, the royal chroniclers arrived. Hernán Cortés himself (1485–1547) wrote *Las cartas de relación,* and Bernal Díaz del Castillo (1492–ca. 1581) describes at length *The True History of the Conquest of Mexico.* Bartolomé de Las Casas (1474–1566), also called the "advocate of the Indians," went public with all the cruelties and abuses the Spaniards had inflicted, and still were inflicting, on the indigenous people with his *Brevísima relación de la destrucción de las Indias* (*A Short Account of the Destruction of the Indies*).

The colonial period included some writers and poets who had been born or had lived most of their lives in Nueva España. The "tenth muse," Sor Juana Inés de la Cruz, wrote immortal verses that are recited every day by women struggling with difficult relationships: *"Hombres necios que acusais...* (Stupid men, you, who accuse . . .)." Besides Juan Ruiz de Alarcón y Mendoza (ca. 1581–1639), who wrote comedies and poems in the traditional Spanish style, there were notable historians who tried to preserve as much as they could of Mexico's history.

The independence movement encouraged some writers to look at their new country with new attitudes—for instance, José Fernández de Lizardi (1776–1827) with *El periquillo sarniento,* or Ignacio Altamirano (1934–1983) with *Navidad en las montañas.* When, at the time of the revolution, Modernism swept through the Americas, Mexico was worried about "tierra y libertad": how to succeed on one side and how to suppress on the other. Mariano Azuela (1873–1952) captures those first years of the revolution in his widely read *Los de abajo.* Other books a Mexican might want to add to her library are *Pedro Páramo* by Juan Rulfo and *El laberinto de soledad* by Nobel laureate Octavio Paz, which held up a mirror that reflects Mexican identity.

After that there remains a long reading list of many more excellent writers who deal with our times and problems in a way unique to Latin-American literature, by suspending reality in imagination—a realm where time has no meaning, physical constraints do not exist, and universal dreams make life livable and beautiful. Contemporary literature follows this path in its examination of life as is, in such **47** works as *Hasta no verte, Jesus mio* by Elena Poniatowska, *Como agua para chocolate* by Laura Esquivel, and *La lluvia de oro* by Victor Villaseñor, a sweeping epic family saga that emphasizes Mexican family values surviving in the cruel migration to the North.

The literary voices within Mexico, as well as those of Mexican writers living in the United States, are getting louder—for those inclined to listen. After all, literature has always accompanied, predicted, and commented on the human condition and protested against threats, from wherever they might come. With the increasing Mexican presence in the United States, the already existing bilingual treasure trove will continue to be used in daily interaction, TV, radio, and literature. Reading Rodolfo Anaya's novel *Bless Me, última,* shows how English and Spanish can really dance with each other.

Related Web link: library.csustan.edu/lboyer/
modern_languages/mexican.htm—articles and
links on Mexican literature (E)

Los mariachis: y la música toca y toca

Mariachi is the best when it comes to giving Mexican culture a voice. Only this music can transmit what it means to be Mexican. Mariachis can bring all the facets of the intricate Mexican soul together and express it in a wide variety of songs: from a hymn to the rejected macho ("El rey," the king) to ballads of famous horses ("El caballo prieto azabache," the black horse), the revolution ("La Adelita"), the bar scene ("El cantinero," the barkeeper), odes to towns or regions ("Guadalajara"), love ("Volver y volver"), farewells ("La golondrina," the swallow), and unconditional patriotism ("Mexico lindo y querido," dear and beautiful Mexico).

A close second to music is the mariachis' spectacular uniform. Tight pants, a belt of intricately woven *maguey* (sisal) fibers, a bolero-type jacket, and the wide-rimmed hat, all richly adorned with silver buttons, ribbons, and chains. These suits quickly identify them as close "relatives" to the *charros*, the gentlemen cowboys. And they do, indeed, have a lot in common, including their origin in Jalisco and neighboring states.

Mariachi bands used to consist of only three or four guitarists playing together for the townspeople at the *quiosco* (gazebo) on the zocalo, the main square. Nowadays, however, there can be up to eighteen musicians with the ability to play *anything*. Besides guitars there are the *vihuelas* (smaller, five-string guitars), *guitarrones* (big-bellied, six-string giant *vihuelas*), harps for the rhythm, violins to carry the tune, and trumpets to set lively accents.

And why the name mariachi? It could be from the French *mariage*, for music traditionally played at weddings. But the consensus nowadays is that mariachis existed long before the French came to Mexico, and the name actually came from an indigenous word *mariache* meaning a small platform big enough for the musicians and some dancing couples.

Where can they be found and heard? Everywhere in Mexico! For a high concentration, there is the famous Plaza Garibaldi in Mexico City, five blocks north of the Latin American Tower, and, of course, in Guadalajara, the Plaza de Los Mariachis (at the intersection of Independencia Sur and Mina). In both plazas visitors can have their own *serenata* for Mex$20 and up per song.

FINE ARTS AND MUSIC
Muralismo

To get the message out, give man a voice—or a blank slate. The urge to communicate with others through visual symbols and clues, to educate them, explain urgent issues, tell stories, enlighten, or even mislead is as deeply ingrained as spoken language.

In Mexico, pyramids were adorned; the Catholic church explained biblical stories through pictures, decorations, statues and sculptures in churches; and the government directs crowds with signs. In Mexico City, for example, transit authorities have assigned a pictograph for every subway station.

After the Mexican Revolution of 1910, in rebuilding society and expanding infrastructure, the walls of public and private buildings offered a unique canvas on which to express a new national conscience and celebrate *el patrimonio* (patriotism and national heritage). When in 1922 José Vasconcelos, Secretary of Education, made Diego Rivera, then already known as a superb painter of frescos, the offer to use the walls of SEP's offices for his art, the *muralismo* movement was born. Without any doubt, it was through this art form that Mexico made its major contribution to contemporary art. Diego Rivera (1886–1957) was the pioneer—very controversial, but at the forefront of the contemporary art scene. In Europe he absorbed everything from the Italian Renaissance to cubism. While his political affiliations with communism caused some to view him negatively, his frank identification with his homeland, its people, and their struggle made him extremely popular. His paintings sometimes seem like overwhelming screams bursting off the walls as they depicted the agonizing history of Mexico from the first cry for independence in 1850 to the constitution of 1917. Representative samples of his murals can be found in the Palacio Nacional, in the Secretaria de Educación in Chapingo, and at Cortés' palace in the town of Cuernavaca.

José Clemente Orozco (1883–1949) is considered by many to represent the pinnacle of the movement. His paintings elevated the struggle to a global level and denounced the horrors of war and social hypocrisy. Some of his major works can be found in the Palacio del Gobierno in Guadalajara.

The third of the great Mexican muralists was David Alfaro Siqueiros (1896–1974), a lifelong social and political activist. His paintings often added a third dimension through integrated sculpture, and appear as an ongoing call for action. He was part of the revolution, later fought in the Spanish Civil War, and stood on the front line with strikers for social causes at home. He also deals with Mexico's history—for example in the castle in Chapultepec Park, the Palacio de Bellas Artes, and La Ciudad Universitaria in Mexico City. His workshop in Cuernavaca holds some unfinished paintings and can still be visited.

Other great muralists include Gerardo Murillo (1875–1974; aka Dr. Atl), who as early as 1904 showed the way by opposing the artistic glorification of the dictator Porfirio Díaz with some scandalous paintings. After Rivera, Orozco, and Siqueiros comes a long list of excellent muralists, including Rufino Tamayo (1899–1991), and eventually a decline, when the initial passion deteriorated into a mere trend.

Related Web link: mcfinland.vassar.edu/demos/ projects/mexicano.html—background and images of significant Mexican muralists (E)

Pyramid of Tulum, Yucatán

Frida (and Diego)

It is outside Mexico that Frida Kahlo became a national icon. Toward the end of the twentieth century, the global art community became infatuated with the art and personal tragedy of Frida and her relationship with Diego Rivera, the most famous of Mexican muralists. This fascination was probably triggered when she stepped out of the enormous shadow that Diego cast over his surroundings as an artist and political force, and indeed in the physical sense—people liked to describe the couple as *la paloma y el elefante* (the dove and the elephant), as she was petite and young while he was huge and twenty years older.

Frida first met Diego as a high school student at the National Preparatory School where he was working on his first government-commissioned mural. She fell in love with him and his work, and probably also his status and political affiliation, even when her friends were in disbelief about her fascination with *este viejo gordo asqueroso* (that disgusting fat old man).

In 1925, at the age of eighteen, Frida was caught in a terrible traffic accident between the school bus she rode and a streetcar. She was impaled by a metal rod and suffered severe multiple fractures in her back, ribs, right leg, collar bone, and pelvis. She made a remarkable recovery, but lived on and off in excruciating pain, both physical and psychological, for the rest of her life. During her long hospital stays Frida started painting as a means to overcome her physical disabilities.

In 1928 Frida and Diego met again, shortly after his marriage had broken up.

Diego, being a *mujeriego* (ladies' man), was flattered by young Frida's infatuation with everything he stood for, and they married on August 21, 1929. What started on that day was anything but marital bliss. For Frida it was a roller-coaster ride of intense creativity, travel, betrayal, international success, infidelity, and excesses; suspicion of participating in Russian Leon Trotsky's assassination; Diego's exile, separation, and divorce; and repeated surgery, remarriage with Diego, and amputation of a leg—all the while celebrating life.

In 1954, the year of her death, she named one of her last paintings "Viva la vida (Long Live Life)." However, the last entry in her diary reads *"el mundo es mejor así...* (the world is better this way . . .)," which has led to speculation of suicide.

The house in Coyoacan where Frida was born is still there. It is now a museum that celebrates her life, passions, and extreme agonies. Her work includes, above all, many self-portraits: "Autoretrato con traje de terciopelo (Self-Portrait in a Velvet Suit)," "Frida Kahlo y Diego Rivera," "Frida y el aborto (Frida and the Abortion)," "Mi nana y yo," "Columna rota (Broken Spine)," "Diego y yo," "Yo y mis pericos (My Parrots and I)," "Las dos Fridas (The Two Fridas)," and many more. These portraits offer a haunting insight into the complexity of who Frida was.

Related Web link: publispain.com/fridakahlo—
biographical information and paintings (S)

Mexican Music

When the music starts playing in Mexico, people will not only listen but will often take it as a signal for *una buena pachanga* (a good party). Not much is needed to celebrate life besides good company, food, and music, which are available anywhere at any time.

Mexican music, no matter what kind, will always trigger instant participation — clapping, singing along, dancing, crying, or *echando un grito del alma*, mostly *el macho* (the man) shouting out a heartfelt yell in the "ai-yaiyai-yai" category, with its delivery directly dependent on the progression of the party or on the presence of a señorita to be impressed.

Worldwide, mariachi bands are probably the best-known representatives of the Mexican musical genre. They enhance every stage and event in life from baptism to funeral. They can be hired for serenades and entertain the crowds at *charreadas* (rodeos) and bullfights, and gladly group around restaurant tables, taking requests from the patrons. They have adapted many kinds of music from many different regions in Mexico, even abroad (for example, "Spanish Eyes," "Cocomo"), and have arranged them in their own style. The mariachi band El Sol de México from Los Angeles, for example, took the popular song "California Girls," turned it into "Acapulco Girls," and then invited the Beach Boys, the original composers, to sing along with them.

Original indigenous music is very much alive. It employs unique instruments made of materials from the natural environment, such as turtle shells, hollowed-out tree stems (called *teponoaxtli* and *huehuetl*), clay, notched bones, and gourds, which provide the rhythm while simple flutes carry the tune. In pre-Columbian times music was mainly performed for religious ceremonies; today it is more for enhancement of tourist sites, but also, polished to perfection, accompanies performances of the Ballet Folklórico at the Palacio de Bellas Artes in Mexico City.

Mexican music is the result of indigenous interaction with the Spanish conquerors and encounters at the northern borders with German, French, English, and Irish immigrants to the United States, and the Caribbean and African imprint drawn from the Gulf of Mexico. On the Pacific coast, from Tierra del Fuego to Las Californias, Spanish galleons gathered and disseminated the music and dances they found on their way. And there were more ethereal influences from the classical European musical scene on well-respected Mexican composers such as Silvestre Revueltas, Carlos Chavez, José Pablo Moncayo, Manuel Ponce, and others.

Many of the popular music forms are homegrown in their particular region. Las Chilenas on the Pacific coast of Guerrero have their roots in *las cuecas* from Chile; *la música tejana* brings in the accordions, rhythm, and sounds of Texas and its multicultural heritage; and *la música norteña* or *la música ranchera* celebrates the cowboy way of life à la country music. *El huapango*, a very mestizo expression of the people of La Huasteca (located on the eastern slopes of the Sierra Madre Oriental toward the coastal plains of the Gulf

Coast), is partially based on challenging impromptu verses flying back and forth between the singers while at the same time dancers try to compete with intricate steps to outlast their opponents. In Pahuatlán de Valle, in the state of Puebla, the *huapango* goes on, night and day, throughout *la Semana Santa* (Easter Week) every year.

Somewhat less extemporaneous, but also made up on the spur-of-the-moment "breaking news," is the *corrido*. Originally a medieval Spanish ballad form, it has become a poetic new-world medium. Itinerant singers disseminated current events by singing their songs on their rounds throughout colonial Nueva España (New Spain), picking their heroes according to popular opinion. These ballads are still the favorite domain of musical groups such as Los Tigres del Norte, Los Tucanes, and others. They have revived a tradition that culminated in the early 1900s during the Mexican Revolution, with classic *corridos* like "Valentín de la Sierra," many about Pancho Villa, as well as dedications to "brave" states ("Corrido de Chihuahua") or exceptional horses ("El caballo blanco"). At present authorities are trying to ban *corridos* that promote the wrong heroes—drug lords and *narco-traficantes*.

Crossing the border, recent *corridos* tell the sad stories about "La tumba del mojado (The Grave of the Wetback)," "El once Negro (9/11)," or dealings with *la migra* and life in *las Califas* (California). But *la música toca y toca...* (the music keeps playing) with romantic songs, boleros, and *valses* (waltzes), a cornucopia of regional songs from every state, *canciones de cuna* (lullabies), and *guaco* rock (contemporary rock) by groups such as Maná, or the music of Santana, originally from Autlán (Jalisco), where his statue graces the town square.

On an all-time Mexican hit parade there are the certain tearjerkers: "Las golondrinas," a farewell song that leaves no eye dry—just like "México lindo y querido." "El rey," by José Alfredo Jiménez which helps the macho indulge in his pain, while "La bamba," originally from the state of Veracruz, has lifted up spirits around the world, as has "El rancho grande" or "Cielito lindo."

Mexican music has a big following all over Latin America. Its infectious quality is not found to such an extent anywhere else. The early mornings belong to "Las mañanitas," the birthday song, and in the later hours, after a hard day's work, people crank up *la música ranchera* while having a few cold ones.

Related Web links: fciencias.unam.mx/ejemplo/ MusicaMex/MusicaMex.html—traditional music (S); lanzadera.com/baldemusic—Mexican music and composers (S), mexconnect.com/mex _/travel/jcar/jcbamba.html—La Bamba explained (E)

Mexican and Latino Stars: Crossing Over

Hollywood has always needed to find the stereotypical Latino lover. One of the first was Rudolph Valentino, who was actually of Italian descent. Since then the American film industry has taken great liberty in casting popular actors into the wrong ethnic roles. But then the same thing has been going on in Latin movies and TV; it is the blond woman who dominates the scene, against all demographic reality! One exception could be Ricardo Montalban, who was born in Mexico and played the Mexican lover for many years before he became a popular TV star ("Fantasy Island") and, in his later years, got to perform in character roles in big Hollywood productions.

To be able to "cross over" the cultural threshold, a star has to be accepted on both sides. The Panamanian actor and activist Rubén Blades portrayed the agony of selling out his own culture for material gain in a movie called *Crossover Dreams* (1985). Similar dilemmas have been faced by the late Selena, who, as a native Texan and U.S. citizen, didn't even fit the immigrant category, but still had to walk across that bridge between languages and cultures within her own country. Julio Iglesias made several attempts to repeat his tremendous success in the Spanish-speaking world in the United States. Even though he sings in many languages, including English, and performed with major U.S. stars such as Willie Nelson, he did not win over the American audience.

Contemporary actors portraying Latin Americans often come from Spanish ancestry rather than from Latin America—

for instance, the versatile Antonio Banderas, Penélope Cruz, and before them Rita Hayworth and Charo. But recently there seems to be an abundance of Latinos making it big time in the United States. A few (Salma Hayek, Cameron Diaz, Jennifer Lopez) have succeeded in the film industry, but the list of musicians and singers goes back further in time and continues to grow in leaps and bounds. Celia Cruz, Santana, Vicky Carr, and Ricky Martin could be considered pioneers who prepared the scene for the likes of Shakira, Christina Aguilera, Marc Anthony, Enrique Iglesias, the rock group Maná, and others.

Living with an increasingly visible presence of Latinos in the United States, the white Anglo-Saxon Protestant population has become used to, and more accepting of, the multicultural experience. To make it as a celebrity it is not necessary to have an English-sounding name. Baseball stars never had to worry about that issue: Sammy Sosa, Rafael Palmeiro, or Juan Gonzalez can prove that.

Even Hollywood would not object to hiring one of the new Latino directors who have more than earned their good reputation—Alfonso Cuarón with the third Harry Potter movie, *The Prisoner of Azkaban*, Fernando Mereilles with *City of God*, and Walter Salles with *The Motorcycle Diaries*.

Related Web links: cinemexicano.mty.itesm.mx/directores/alfonso_cuaron.html—Alfonso Cuarón filmography (S); us.imdb.com/name/nm0001544—Ricardo Montalban filmography (E)

Dance

The salsa, the merengue, and *la cumbia* are popular dances throughout Latin America and the Caribbean. There are *discotecas* everywhere for any kind of music, not just the Latino scene. The younger crowd tends to listen and dance to popular American music but does not exclude their own. Dancing is also a very common pastime at any kind of fiesta, and on weekends local communities organize *bailes* (dances) in central plazas or *salas de baile* (dance halls). The DJ's music selection depends very much on the region. In the rural areas, *la música norteña* or *ranchera* or *la banda* (small brass bands) tend to be very popular. The dance steps follow a simple march or polka type rhythm, and once in a while a new dance is "it." For a while *la quebradita* was in and went well with the *banda* music from the state of Sinaloa. Then came *el pasito duranguense* from the state of Durango, and sometimes a special song comes along with its very own dance, as did *la macarena, la bomba* (from Colombia),

and "Aserejé," a song from Spain that actually went all around the world one summer. Along the Rio Grande, *conjuntos tejanos*, with accordions in their bands, will get everybody dancing the polka. Metropolitan discos often have live music performing any style of international music, from heavy metal to alternative.

Los bailes tradicionales (traditional dance) are not for participation, but rather performed for ceremonial purposes on very specific occasions in certain places only. Usually, the dancers line up in front of the church and, through their dance movements and mime, sometimes narration, tell of historical events or perform rituals that go back to pre-Columbian times. Missionaries often used dance to explain biblical details.

Los Santiagos are a good example. They reenact the defeat of *los moros* during the times of the reconquest of Spain. The Santiagos, representing the Christian army, have white mock horses tied to their belts

Palacio de Bellas Artes, D.F.

and fiercely attack the moors, the Islamic forces that occupied Spain A.D. 711–1492. In this dance the Santiagos completely defeat *los moros* and convert them to Christianity.

La danza de los Quetzales (dance of the Quetzal bird) in Cuetzalán, shows, in colorful costumes and feathery headdresses, the path of the sun across the skies. In Michoacán, around Lake Patzcuaro, *los viejitos* (the little old men), played by young men wearing wooden masks and white peasant's outfits, prove that supposedly decrepit old people can still do vigorous dances.

Masks play a special role in numerous Mexican dances. A dancer can become anything he needs to be, from a ferocious animal to a scary supernatural being. *Los bailarines tigres* (tiger dancers) from the state of Guerrero demonstrate the campesino's deep fear of wild animals and other things that lurk out there in the dark.

La danza de la Malinche, in the state of San Luis Potosí, acts out the story of Cortés and La Malinche, his translator and, later on, mistress. In her dance she shows regret and shame for betraying her own people. And the list goes on, one ethnic group after the other: the deer and coyote dances of the Yaquis, the *negritos* dance of the Totonacos in Veracruz, the ribbon dances of the Maya in Yucatán, and so on.

El jarabe tapatio from Jalisco, also known as the Mexican Hat Dance, is probably *the* most popular national secular folk dance, followed closely by the *Huapangos* from the Huastecas, the eastern slopes of the Sierra Madre Oriental, the states of

Tamaulipas, Hidalgo, and Veracruz. *Huapangos* are events that can go on for days and through the nights. Musical groups alternate, bringing on a variety of improvised verses and a different *son* (tune), as young men and women show their endurance and skills in complicated *zapateados* (tap dancing steps) that provide a steady rhythm for the violins and guitars. *Huapangos* can happen anywhere at any time, at weddings, or at other fiestas that are not connected to the church. All that is needed is a wooden platform, a few musicians, and *mucha cerveza*!

To get a good idea of many different folk dances without trying to find the places of origin, visit La Guelaguetza (a statewide gathering of ethnic groups performing their dances) in Oaxaca during the third and fourth weeks of July. Dancers in their colorful *trajes típicos* (local costumes) convene and perform their authentic dances from all regions of Oaxaca. The state of Puebla has a similar yearly event, the Atlixcáyotl, on the last Sunday in September in the town of Atlixco. The dances here include the famous *voladores* (the flying men).

For the complete picture, it is a must to go to a performance of the famous Ballet Folklórico de Mexico in the Palacio de Bellas Artes in the capital. The two-hour show is a dazzling fiesta of lights, color, music, and professional dancers.

Related Web link: mexfoldanco.org—information on dances from Mexican Folkloric Dance Company, Chicago (E, S)

Papel amate: More than Something to Write On

In the last years of the reign of Montezuma II (1466–1520), the papermakers of the Aztec empire had to pay their annual tribute of 480,000 sheets of paper. The paper was used in religious ceremonies, as ornaments hung around the idols on certain feast days, and, on some occasions as part of the high priests' vestments. A great amount was used for "books"—actually sheets glued together, folded like a fan, and then painted with hieroglyphic texts. After the conquest imported paper from Europe eventually replaced the Aztec paper and the art of papermaking was forgotten—as was the case in the small town of Tepoztlan near Cuernavaca. Only in some remote areas of the Huasteca (the eastern slope of the Sierra Madre) in the northern parts of the states of Puebla and Veracruz has the art survived over the centuries, mostly because until recently many places were accessible only by *caminos de herradura* (arduous horse trails).

Two villages in particular have made paper continually since pre-Columbian times: in the Xicotepec region, Veracruz, with a population of Aztec origin, is one, and San Pablito (Puebla), an Otomí Indian village, is the other. San Pablito is nowadays within easy reach of the Mexico City area. About twenty years ago a gravel road reached the village and connected it with "civilization," but paper is still made in the old way. Men bring in strips of bark from the mulberry tree (for whitish paper) and the wild fig (for dark-brown paper). The inner bark is peeled off and handed over to the women. In big kettles of water, mixed with ashes of wood, they boil the bark until it is soft and rinse it in cold water. The moist fibers are laid out in a crisscross pattern on a smooth board and pounded with a flat stone until all the strands are felted together. After drying in the sun the sheets can easily be lifted off the boards.

Most of the finished product ends up in souvenir stores brightly painted with floral or Aztec motives as *papel amate*, a word derived from the Aztec *amatl* meaning "fig tree." Some of it goes to Amayaltepec (Guerrero), where the local artists established a tradition of depicting scenes from everyday Mexican life. And, not officially accounted for, a considerable amount is used in the *curanderos'* healing ceremonies and black magic.

Related Web link: muertos.palomar.edu/muertos links.htm#Papel—links for *papel amate* (S)

La China Poblana: The Mexican-Chinese Connection

The Puebla state museum displays a treasured costume—a long red-flannel skirt trimmed with sequins, the upper part green, worn with a white embroidered blouse, a rebozo hanging over the shoulders and crossed in front with beaded strings attached all over, and a bow of colored ribbons for the hair. It is the dress of the legendary China Poblana, the Chinese lady from Puebla.

How did she get to Puebla, and why that national recognition? Historical evidence is scarce. For one, it is a story that highlights the early trade patterns of colonial New Spain with the Far East. As the sea routes were established around Cape Horn, up to Acapulco, then on to Manila in the Philippines and beyond, they also instantly attracted pirates.

By the late 1600s Spanish supply ships, or vessels bringing back the treasures from the colonies, moved through heavily infested corsair territories. Among the bounty of one of the raids there was a beautiful young Chinese princess, who was sold in Acapulco as a slave to a Captain Miguel Sosa from Puebla. He saw to it that she was treated decently, had her baptized, and changed her name from Mirrha of the kingdom of Indra Prashta to Catarina de San Juan. Father Aguila, her mentor, described her as "one of the loveliest and most perfect beauties of her day. Her skin was light rather than dark, her hair blond, she had a high forehead, bright eyes, straight nose, and the rest of her features was in perfect harmony with the graceful

elegance of her body and to all of this was added her strong desire to preserve her purity." She became a devout Catholic and a model for the virtuous ladies of the city of Puebla. No wonder they all wanted to imitate her and wear the exotic clothes that she had managed to re-create from local materials.

So it came that many folkloric dance troupes adopted that particular costume nationwide. A visit of the Palacio de Bellas Artes in Mexico City or a performance of a ballet folklórico in Guadalajara will allow the visitor to admire a variety of versions of the famous costume of the China Poblana.

Related Web link: ifccsa.org/poblano.html—picture of the famous costume of the China Poblana (E)

La danza de los voladores

The dance itself is not so unusual. The men's movements and their toe-and-heel tapping are a common sight and sound at folkloric events throughout Mexico. That the *capitán* (lead man) is playing both a flute and a small handheld drum as he leans forward and slowly turns around to the rhythm of his own music isn't extraordinary either. But the fact that he is about 30 m (90 ft) above the ground, performing his dance on a tiny wooden platform that rotates on top of a wooden pole, definitely is. And this happens simultaneously with the spiraling flight of four men hanging by their feet from ropes that slowly unwind as the dancers complete thirteen circles before they touch the ground. The men symbolize sacred flying creatures guarding the four points of the compass for the year to come (4 men × 13 circles each = 52!), most likely to ask the gods for rain, sun, and a plentiful harvest.

The tradition of the *voladores* (pole flyers) is very much alive in the Huasteca region, the eastern slopes of the Sierra Madre that includes the coastal plains of Veracruz. The principal ethnic group to perform the ceremony are the Totonac Indians, who claim it is in their blood. The *danza de los voladores* had, however, traditionally been practiced by other tribes as far south as Nicaragua.

Los voladores de Papantla (a town in the state of Veracruz) seem to have preserved and cultivated the tradition more than anybody else and lately even monopolized it. In the 1970s the *voladores* organized and formed a union. They also established a school for *la formación* (edu-

cation and training) of the next generation of fliers.

The local leaders are keenly aware of the commercial potential of their performances and therefore always emphasize the spiritual and religious background of pole flying. All too often greedy intermediaries have turned the *voladores*' performance into meaningless, albeit spectacular, circus acts plagued by tragic accidents. At some point authorities had to step in to protect the cultural heritage of the indigenous people.

To see an authentic *volador* performance, the annual fair in Papantla (Veracruz), around the Corpus Christi celebrations in spring might be the place, as would be the nearby archaeological site of El Tajín. Another picturesque village in the mountains of Puebla state, Cuetzalán, hosts performances around the same time. "Shows" right in front of the anthropological museum in Mexico City still have a feeling of authenticity because of the context the museum provides. Nowadays the Fondo Nacional del Turismo (FONATUR) also gives its blessing to performances in tourist resorts, controlling the setting and guaranteeing the dignity of the performers of the Papantla school—even if resort managers might hope that the ceremony has all but lost one of its original purposes: that of bringing rain!

Related Web links: kivu.com/multimedia/ mexindians.html (E); baxtion.com/mx/los%20 _voladores_de_papantla.htm (S)—photos of voladores de Papantla

60

La Llorona: Where Are My Children?

Huddling around a campesino's fireplace on a cold dark night might just be the right setting to hear about La Llorona, the weeping woman. She appears, they say, to unsuspecting villagers who are out and about past the expected hours, often on the way home from work in the field, enjoying *la pulquería*, a happy gathering of compadres, or a chat with *las vecinas* (neighbor ladies).

From the southwestern states of the U.S., throughout Mexico, and all the way to Central America people swear they have run at one time or another into a woman dressed in flowing black robes, a shawl shadowing her face, who walks along rivers, creeks, *acequias* (ditches), and lakeshores wailing incessantly, "*¡Ayiii de mis hijos!* (Oh, what about my children!)" Then, they say, it is best to run for shelter and close doors and windows tightly. Even the bravest of dogs come running home whimpering with their tail between their legs because nobody has ever lived to describe her face.

Who is she? Within the many regionally different plots of the story lies one recurring horrid theme: that of a mother drowning her own children, after being abandoned by their father, and eventually killing herself. Unable to find rest, she haunts waterways searching for the souls of her dead children.

Regional lore often paints different backgrounds to this basic myth. In the deserts of New Mexico, for example, the father is a rich farmer's son who betrays Maria and the children. One of the many typical *acequias* becomes the setting for the legend. In some of the Mexican versions the plot often goes back to the early days of New Spain. In one, a Spanish *hidalgo* (nobleman) is the father, and his mistress, the unfortunate native mother, is left behind with their offspring as he pursues his military career in other places.

The most popular version, however, draws two protagonists of the conquest, Hernán Cortés and his mistress, Doña Marina (La Malinche), into the plot. Vaguely supported by historical events that legends are usually based on, Doña Marina pleads with Cortés to take her and the children back to Spain with him. He rejects the idea as absurd, because of the way Spaniards look at the natives. When he leaves Tenochtitlán for a visit to Spain, she kills the children before his eyes as he passes in a ceremonial parade and waves at them. Then she runs down to the Lake of Texcoco that used to surround the city and disappears in the dark waters—only to come back to haunt errant wanderers so much that they might even give up drinking and carousing for the rest of their lives.

Related Web link: literacynet.org/lp/hper spectives/llorona.html—another version of the legend of La Llorona (E)

Superstitions

"*En martes ni te cases ni embarques* (On Tuesdays neither get married nor go on a trip)" is a popular saying that puts a hex on every single Tuesday—even worse when it falls on the 13th of a month. Then, bad luck might multiply by running into a *pelirrojo* (a redhead), spilling salt or getting *el mal de ojo* (the evil eye), inadvertently or intentionally.

In terms of other superstitions, the rural population seems particularly susceptible to *sustos y espantos* (scares), physical or emotional, or *envidia* (ill will or envy). Resulting sickness, loss of appetite and energy, headaches, or any other psychosomatic symptoms can only be healed by a good *curandera/o*. A cure might come from a wide array of medicinal herbs and plants, *una buena limpia* (a good cleansing/ sweeping ceremony), or an outright reverse *maldición* (voodoo-type curse) on the source of the evil, performed by a *brujo/a* (witch). *Curanderos* also have the power to bring back a lost love or to guarantee a good harvest.

A typical "imported" European superstition, *el corriente del aire, mal aire*, or *vientos* (air drafts, bad air, or winds) might, according to popular belief, bring about pneumonia or worse. Many aches and pains and general energy loss is often and readily diagnosed as a case of *bilis* (bile attack), just as the French are quick to blame the liver (*crise de foie*).

In Mexico, superstitions and belief in the supernatural have always been around and they are often tied to religion, indigenous and Catholic. Whereas the Anglo-Saxon culture tries to control life by taking the right and prudent precautions ("better safe than sorry"), the Latin and indigenous cultures of Mexico take rather the fatalistic attitude of "*que será, será* (what will be, will be)"—the future is beyond human control. It can come only from such supernatural forces as, for example, Tlaloc (the Aztec rain god) all the way to Catholic saints. San Antonio, for example, will protect the traveler and find lost keys, San José keeps an eye on all carpenters, lovers have San Valentín, murderers have San Julian, and all of Mexico has, of course, La Virgen de Guadalupe as the most powerful of all intercessors.

The night usually brings out the "best" of primeval fears: *el coco* or *cucuy* (the bogeyman) for *los escuintles* (the little ones), *el chupacabras* (goatsucker) for the campesinos, and numerous OVNI (UFO) sightings for everybody. Actually, all over the Americas cab drivers seem to be anxious to take you to the scorched landing sites in remote places—or readily point out extraterrestrials mingling with the crowd.

But not to worry: a black cat licking and cleaning itself will give ample warning of any unpleasant surprise or imminent danger ahead.

Related Web link: augustobriga.net/memoria/ supersticiones.htm—Mexican superstitions (S)

El maíz

Corn constitutes the bulk of the three most important basic foods coming out of Mesoamerica: *maíz, frijoles* (beans), and some kinds of *calabaza* (squash). The original wild corn that was domesticated by the first settlers around four thousand years ago came from many different varieties. The corn cultivated today is the result of long crossbreeding and has totally replaced its once wild-growing cousins.

How interdependent and inseparable corn and humans have become is stressed by the fact that corn cannot reseed itself without human intervention. On the one hand the cobs are so tightly covered with husks that they must be shucked to allow reseeding, and on the other humankind could not have survived without corn in the northern parts of the Americas. There are many references to corn in mythology. Some of the cultures actually referred to themselves as *la gente del maíz* (corn people). Archaeologists have proven that every single one of the great cultures was wholly dependent on *maíz*. And people from Mexico to Panama still are; for example, for Mexico the statistics show a yearly consumption of about four hundred pounds per person. That is more than one pound per day!

Maíz is mainly consumed in the form of tortillas and tortilla-based dishes, but there are hundreds of other ways to use *la masa* (cornmeal dough). For special occasions families often prepare tamales. A handful of masa is rolled around some *carne deshebrada* (shredded meat) or *dulces* (candy) and then wrapped in soaked *hojas de maíz* (dried corn husks) and finally boiled for a few hours. Further, *atole* is a thick drink made of corn. Corn on the cob, boiled, dipped, or rubbed with different condiments is a favorite fast food. In markets, campesinos sometimes sell *huitlacoche*, a black fungus that grows on corn in the rainy season. This pre-Columbian mushroom-flavored delicacy can be eaten, for example, with eggs.

Apart from food, *maíz* has a prominent place in legend, indigenous religion, art, *las artesanías*, language, and folklore. As an agricultural commodity, corn plays an important role in the economy from transportation to industrial products such as *almidón* (starch), *jarabe* (syrup), *aceite* (oil), and *gasohol*. As *dextrosa* it finds its way into many lists of ingredients for food products as well as drugs.

Related Web link: mexico.udg.mx/cocina/maiz/ f-maiz.html—uses of corn (S)

Más vale tortillita dura que hambre pura:
Better a Hard Tortilla than Nothing

Created by the ancient people of Mexico, the tortilla has nurtured Mexican life ever since. The patting sound of masa being shaped into perfect rounds has been the telluric rhythm of life for thousands of years in *el hogar* (home, hearth) and has had a deep impact on popular culture.

While the conquering Spaniards succeeded in changing the Mexican indigenous life radically in many areas, their introduction of *harina* (mostly wheat flour) in the tortilla production took hold only where the campesinos could not maintain their *milpa* because of the adverse climate. Today, flour tortillas are used mainly in northern Mexico and the United States, where they can simply take the place of white bread.

Tortillerías (tortilla factories) have all but taken over the bulk production of tortillas in urban areas. Nonetheless, they cannot quite yet replace the home-made tortillas that many a housewife still prepares daily. In the evening *la señora* puts the corn to soak. Next morning the softened kernels, which have started to sprout, are boiled with chunks of lime. She then grinds that corn on a *metate* (mortar) or takes it to a neighborhood *molino* (mill). The resulting *nixtamal*, the masa, is shaped by hand or tortilla press and baked on the hot *comal* (tin, iron, or ceramic griddle), the center of kitchen activities.

Right then, the connoisseur swears, is the best time for a classic taco—tortillas wrapped around a variety of fillings: *frijoles, de olla* (boiled) or *refritos* (refried), a few slices of *aguacate* (avocado), leftover meat or *queso* (cheese), all spiced up with some *salsa casera* (homemade salsa) that usually contains enough chile to complete a nutritious snack.

Tortillas are also fried into hard shells or tortilla chips; they can serve as a plate (as in tostadas), be cut up for a tasty tortilla soup, or become popular casseroles (e.g., *chilaquiles* or a variety of enchilada dishes). In rural areas, tortillas are often the only eating utensil for scooping up food besides a blue-speckled enameled spoon. Some regions have created their very own approaches to the tortilla. In the city of Puebla, for example, *chalupas* (boats) are baked in smaller but thicker patties with beans and salsa spread over the top rather than stuffed inside as in *gorditas* (little fat ones), *huaraches* (shoe shaped), or *sopes* (soups) somewhere else.

The versatility of tortillas has quickly made it a popular food in other cultures because of its convincing health food appeal. The United States, according to Tortilla Industry Association statistics, consumed about two hundred billion tortillas in 2000. It is not hard to believe then, that even John Glenn, on his return to space, insisted on taking along a day's supply of corn tortillas!

Related Web link: public.iastate.edu/~rjsalvad/ scmfaq/tortilla.html#lexicon—how to make tortillas from scratch, comprehensive Nahuatl terminology, recipes (E)

Tequila, *Mezcal*, and Pulque: Where Water Meets Fire

It was a long journey from Tequila (Jalisco) to Jimmy Buffet's Margaritaville—but a successful one: a statement that the current thirty-five producers of the potent drink in the Guadalajara region would easily agree with. Tequila, they will continue, captures the essence of Mexico.

While on one hand the Spanish conquistadors tumbled the Aztec idols down the pyramids, on the other they eagerly embraced the refined pleasures of Aztec nobility. After the thirsty soldiers had exhausted their limited supply of Spanish wine and brandy, they found the holy and strictly ritual drink of pulque, a low-grade alcoholic drink made from the maguey plant, which belongs to the agave family. Abuse of this "holy" drink by commoners used to bring on instant capital punishment. In folk medicine pulque was also widely used for healing purposes by priests and *curanderos*. Its nutritional values are still well known today. According to a popular quote, "*al pulque le falta el hueso para ser carne* (pulque just lacks the bone for being meat)."

Pulque, in the long run, proved to be too weak for the hard-drinking conquistadors. Recognizing the potential of the maguey, they boiled and mashed it and let it ferment. The distilled product, albeit crude, served the purpose. As necessity is the mother of invention, so is the refinement of a product. Production of the *aguardiente* (burning/firewater) became very selective among the different species of maguey, of which only a few guaranteed a satisfactory distillate.

Mezcal used to be the common term for all these varying products of the many different magueys growing throughout the Mexican highlands. But it was the *Agave tequilana* that was eventually singled out in 1902 by a European botanist, Franz Weber, as *the* best raw material for a fine *mezcal*. This the town of Tequila had known since 1873, and they cashed in on its name recognition throughout the twentieth century so that *mezcal* from Tequila became *tequila*! The Sauza family, which has been in the business since 1873, is still producing thirty-five thousand gallons of 90 proof tequila a day, relying on their 155,000 acres of agave plantations. It takes about ten pounds of the core of the maguey, plus a little bit of mashed sugarcane, to get one quart of tequila. This, and the fact that the maguey plant takes about ten years to mature, explains the "bottleneck" the tequila industry went through in the 1990s: increased demand for their product, but not enough plants ready to be processed.

But there's proverbial help:

Para el cruel destino, vino.	For cruel fate, wine.
Para el fracaso, de tequila un vaso.	For failure, a glass of tequila.
Para la tristeza, cerveza.	For sadness, beer.
Para todo mal, mezcal.	For everything bad, mezcal.

Related Web links: itequila.org (E), cuervo.com (E, S); linox.itgo.com—more information about tequila (S)

Caterpillars and Grasshoppers: Adventures in Food

Probably the best-known Mexican culinary peculiarity abroad is the "worm" that comes along within a bottle of *mezcal*, the potent drink of Oaxaca. While it lends a nice earthy flavor to the drink, it is rarely eaten once the bottle is empty.

Available in markets of southern Mexico, this worm is called *gusano de maguey* (agave caterpillar), a shrimplike creature that is indeed consumed air-dried, toasted plain, or wrapped in a tortilla. That is also true for sun-dried or fried *chapulines* (grasshoppers), a crunchy specialty of Oaxaca that may turn up with salt and lime as a *botana* (appetizer) to go with a drink.

The infamous chocolate-covered ants, however, might be culinary fiction, but close enough: the rendered fat of big, plump *hormigas* (ants), called *chicantanas* in the border regions of Chiapas and Veracruz, is used during the rainy season for a popular salsa called *tlatonile*. Fried *hormigas* are said to taste like popcorn.

On the back roads of the states of Guerrero and Morelos, *jumiles* (stinkbugs) fill regional tacos either alive or smothered in salsa. Then there is also a Mexican version of escargot, the *caracol*: snails anywhere might be cooked in red or green *mole* just like iguanas. According to folk medicine, the meat of these friendly lizards strengthens lungs and helps convalescents on the road to recovery. Similar properties are attributed to the *ajolote* (*axolotl*), a salamander that lingers in its embryonic state. *Ajolotes* can be found in the markets of the Tlaxcala/Puebla region alive, as *the* main ingredient of *ajolote* broth, or further processed into a tonic comparable to cod liver oil. Equally exotic seem to be other meat sources like the armadillo, eaten with *adobo* (spicy red chile sauce), or other small mammals, the *mapache*, *tlacuache*, *tejón* (badger), and even *zorillo* (skunk).

Because of their limited seasonal availability, all those regional rarities have probably attained a status far beyond their culinary merits. They always have been, as research maintains, the poor man's answer in the search for protein—a quest that centuries ago, according to some archaeologists, might ultimately have driven the Aztecs to cannibalism.

In spite of the low appeal of insects and other nontraditional animals in mainstream culture, the ever-growing quest to feed humankind around the globe has prompted the Instituto de Biología of UNAM to take a serious second look at these unusual food sources for their possible nutritional value.

Jumil (stinkbug), a Guerrero delicacy

Related Web links: uky.edu—information on "bug food" (E); suite101.com/article.cfm/ enabling_garden/78206—on entomological epicurean delights (E)

Eating Out: Appetite Without Angst

One of the tourist's challenges while exploring is to resist the constant aroma of food drifting through the air. But while everything *smells* so delicious, it usually comes with the agony of, "Can my stomach take it?" Tourists always come more than well warned of "Montezuma's revenge," and often with a good supply of pills "just in case." Basic precaution is good, but not overreacting is even better. Almost doing as the Mexicans do is best.

Thirsty? Don't look for water fountains, but choose instead from an array of bottled *refrescos*, from the familiar Coca-Cola, Sprite, and Fanta, to Agua Tehuacán (mineral water from the city of Tehuacán), Sidral Mundet (an apple soda), and many more. The key word, however, remains "bottled." The selection for the dehydrated traveler continues with some excellent *cervezas* and *vino doméstico, tinto o blanco* (red or white domestic wine), or *cocteles* (mixed drinks) with tequila, *ron* (rum) *doméstico*, or many other kinds of *aguardiente* (firewater).

Should the delicious aroma of food still be around, the source might be the many food stalls in the market you just explored. Find one with many customers and have a solid *desayuno* (breakfast) of *huevos rancheros* or *huevos a la mexicana* (ranch- or Mexican-style eggs, both served with tortillas and plenty of salsa) with a good cup of *café con leche* (often instant Nescafé with hot milk). Dip a *pan dulce* (a sweet roll) into that coffee. Compliment the cook with *"¡Qué rico!* (How tasty!)" This should last you until lunch around midafternoon.

By then, you might be drawn into one of the many small restaurants offering a *comida corrida*, a set daily menu of three courses, probably with *sopa de fideos* (noodle soup) and a main dish with some kind of *carne* (meat). Tortillas and *frijoles* as well as a *postre* (desert) such as *flan* (caramel custard) are most likely included.

During afternoon activities and/or siestas, good snacks include anything wrapped—*galletas* (cookies, crackers), any fruit that you can peel yourself, *dulces* (sweets, candies), and *bebidas embotelladas* (bottled drinks).

La cena (dinner) will be served late, often around 10 o'clock. The variety of food available in the different regions of Mexico is huge, and the basic precautions remain a reality whether eating at a neighborhood restaurant or the fancy international resort. Drink *agua purificada*, be critical of the *lechuga* (green salad), trust your senses, and try to follow your regular eating habits as much as possible. And don't forget to wish *"¡Buen provecho!* (Enjoy your meal!)" to all the people around your table!

Related Web link: spanish.about.com/cs/travel/a/travel_vocab.htm—useful vocabulary for eating out (E)

Chiles: Some Like It Hot

"**N**o tengas miedo al chile, aunque lo veas colorado (Don't be afraid of the chile even though you see it is red)" is the proverbial Mexican advice, taking deceiving appearances to the culinary level. After all, the chile that might look too *picante* (hot, stinging) could still be *sabroso* (tasty). Finding the balance between too hot and still tasting good could be a rewarding project for the occasional traveler. Opportunities for field studies abound, from streamlined supermarkets and upscale restaurants in Chicago to open-air markets in Chiapas and its hidden-away *fondas* (eating stalls).

El chile is *muy mexicano*. It had been cultivated for thousands of years before Cortés introduced it to the Old World. Seeds of these "new" plants were pushed into the ground everywhere, and it soon was discovered that the shape, size, and "hotness" of the chile depend on many different ecological circumstances. This is the main reason why scientific studies of the "hotness factor" have been so difficult. Macho assertions of maximum tolerance levels are as deceiving as the desperate gasps of a victim of a chile attack.

A variety of methods to determine pungency have been developed. Subjectively they all rely on the taste buds of the testing group. The Scoville test takes a semiscientific approach, relying on tasting and controlled sequences of the taster's sensitivity. Objectively there is only one, the somewhat costly High-Performance Liquid Chromatography (HPLC). This one gets down to measure the heat of the chile as well as the amount of the capsaicinoids.

The good old scale from 1 to 100 is still around. It maintains that at between 55 and 60 the human taste buds are rendered useless or, possibly, destroyed.

From all these different methods arises one rather uniform consensus of ranking the most popular chiles like this (10 is the hottest):

bell pepper	0
yellow wax	1
guajillo, Anaheim	2–3
cherry, Poblano	3
jalapeño	4
ancho	5
chipotle	6
chile de árbol, aji rojo, serrano	7–8
cayenne, piquin, tepin	8
tabasco	9
habanero	10

In the meantime, in millions of Mexican kitchens, chile pods are still being chopped, ground, soaked, peeled, deveined, stuffed, dried, even smoked, confirming Bartolomé de Las Casas's observation in the fifteenth century, "*Sin chile, no creen que estan comiendo* (Without chile, they don't think they are eating)." Chiles continue posing burning questions to the cook and client as well: "How hot is hot enough?"

Related Web links: chilepepperinstitute.org/ pungency.htm—measuring pungency in chiles (E); faxsa.com.mx/semhort1/c60ch001.htm— pictures and information on cultivation (S)

Regional Cuisine

Abroad, Mexican cuisine is often and unjustly reduced to the internationally known and U.S.-palate-approved TexMex repertoire of tacos, enchiladas, bean burritos, salsas, and other similar "streamlined" fast-food items. Although these belie the immense variety of regional dishes, they could be considered the traditional common denominator throughout Mexico.

The meals served at Montezuma's court had Cortés dictate to his historians, "There are so many new and different kinds of vegetables, fruit, and dishes of a variety never seen and names never before pronounced by the likes of us. . . ."

Thus, the conqueror had arrived at yet another challenge, the unique Mexican food pyramid. And the Spaniards got quickly hooked on chocolate, pulque, tomates, *aguacates*, tortillas, *guajolotes*, *frijoles*, and the rest of the fare available in the central valley.

Now, five hundred years later, regional cooking has survived and prospered. Although fundamental improvements in infrastructure (e.g., transportation) have brought in influences from other national regions and from abroad, there is still a wide variety of dishes that depends primarily on the major regional products.

A sampling of Mexico's *cocina regional* (regional cuisine) could start in Baja California with a hearty *sopa de caguama* (turtle stew), to be continued in Guadalajara with a tasty *birria* (steam-baked goat or lamb), topped with a *desempance* (digestive) of smooth *tequila añejo* before moving on down to the coast for either a fresh *huachinango al mojo de ajo* (red snapper fried in a bed of garlic) or the specialty of Guerrero, the *pozole verde* (pork/hominy soup/stew). *Tacos de chapulines* (grasshoppers) in Oaxaca and some baked *robalo en yerba santa* (sea bass) in Chiapas will tie you over for the rest of the culinary conquest by state: *huevos motuleños* (eggs Yucatán style), *jaibas en chilpachole* (crab Veracruz) prepared with *epazote* (worm seed), *carne asada a la tampiqueña* (beef filet of Tampico, Tamps.), *cabrito al horno* (baked kid goat) in Nuevo León, *venado a la serrana* (venison with red chile) in Chihuahua. Then on to *tatishuile* (Mexcaltitlán-style shrimps in corn dough) in Nayarit, picking up some fresh strawberries in Irapuato (Guanajuato), then *taquitos de carnitas* and *barbacoa en mixiote* (barbecued meat wrapped in maguey) in Querétaro, before assaulting Puebla, the stronghold of Mexican cuisine. *Mole poblano* (thick cocoa/chile/everything sauce) originates there as does *chiles en nogada* (a delicate walnut/chile/pomegranate/walnut sauce dish) showing off the red, white, and green of the national flag.

Mexico City, finally, will conclude the culinary tour by either bringing the traveler back into the fold of secure international cuisine and a big selection of fast food, or sending him off into barrios, markets, and side streets to find the ultimate *manjar* (delicacy) of any of the regions, all well represented in the capital.

Related Web links: mexconnect.com/mex_/recipes/foodindex.html (E, S); mexicanfood.about.com/cs/regional (E)—regional recipes and descriptions

El señor presidente, or the Inside Game

Generations of Mexicans lived for decades under the rigid rule of the PRI and under its presidents, but at the beginning of the new millennium developments show a slow but steady move toward more transparency in the political process and toward democracy. What the country wants beyond that, and has been waiting for, is more economic stability, more economic growth, and a better distribution of wealth. All of which the PRInosauro (the established ruling-party-saurus) will not be able or willing to deliver immediately. The president is still very much the spokesperson for the "good old boys."

The wall around that exclusive club, however, is crumbling. The information age and multinational involvements such as NAFTA will eventually drive a wedge into the wheels of the status quo. Not only will the political process but also the people's accepting attitudes (*acceptitudes*) have to change. For most of the twentieth century the population had been excluded from education, access to modern amenities, and any meaningful decision-making processes.

According to the constitution the president is elected by popular vote (unlike in the United States) and can serve only one 6-year term. This system has operated smoothly and uninterruptedly since the Revolutionary Renewal in 1934, when Lázaro Cárdenas assumed the presidency and the PRI gained its prolongued foothold on the political scene in Mexico. Ávila Camacho (1940–1946), Alemán Valdés (1946–1952), Ruiz Cortines (1952–1958), López Mateos (1958–1964), Díaz Ordaz (1964–1970), Echeverría Álvarez (1970–1976), López Portillo (1976–1982), Madrid Hurtado (1982–1988), Salinas de Gortari (1988–1994), and Zedillo Ponce de León (1994–2000), then succeeded each other in the orderly fashion of party tradition, where the next president was handpicked by the acting president's *dedazo* (a tap on the shoulder for the chosen party member) rather than the "elections" offered to a lethargic populace. "Whoever I vote for doesn't matter; the PRI candidate will win anyway," said many a disillusioned citizen and abstained from voting in the last presidential election in 1994.

In 2000, however, a wavering *dedazo* could not send the PRI candidate to the presidential palace at Los Pinos, the president's official residence in Chapultepec Park in Mexico City. It was Vicente Fox, a U.S.-educated businessman from the state of Guanajuato, who, after seventy years of PRI dominance, succeeded in winning a much scrutinized democratic election for his Partido Acción Nacional (PAN, National Action Party).

Experts agree that it is not about *breaking* the PRI's long-term stabilizing power, which still holds a majority throughout the government, but rather a matter of carefully and slowly *shaking off* its iron grip on the country—"¡Viva la democracia!" rather than another bloody revolution.

Related Web link: presidencia.gob.mx—more about the Mexican presidency (S)

El gobierno

Government and politics are something most Mexicans disregard. For them it all happens somewhere in a different universe, with no meaning or effect on everyday life. "If voting would change anything, they wouldn't let us vote anyway" had been the attitude of about 75 percent of the population for the seventy years of PRI politics. *El dedazo* of the president and his cabinet outweighed any opposition or doubt. Mock campaigns, mock elections, and meaningless speeches created the facade of democracy when really it was only about maintaining the status quo — enriching the super rich.

But in the 1990s people started getting restless. Internet access, although scarce, was quickly embraced by the rebels of the Zapatista movement in the southern states. Subcomandante Marcos going online to explain the problems of the people in the state of Chiapas mustered immediate international support and prevented a major military crackdown. Also, NAFTA was about to be signed, a fact that demanded additional transparency in government affairs. The challenge brought on by Vicente Fox from the PAN in the 2000 election, rendered *el dedazo* meaningless, even had Ernesto Zedillo, the outgoing president, wished to use it. And it didn't matter that the PAN is actually more conservative than the PRI; *change* did matter.

The current constitution was proclaimed in 1917; since then politicians have cited it for propaganda purposes while being unwilling to live up to its content. It is considered one of the most radical and comprehensive constitutions in modern history. It wants to ensure national autonomy, social justice, individual rights, and an eight-hour workday; protect women and children; and establish the principle of equal pay for equal work, no matter gender, race, or ethnicity — and much more.

Mexico, officially Los Estados Unidos Mexicanos (the United Mexican States), is a federal republic of thirty-one states and the Distrito Federal (Mexico City). The president, elected for one 6-year term, holds nearly unchecked power, leading critics to call it the "6-year monarchy." But this is not quite true for Mr. Fox. While he managed to get elected in 2000 as a PAN candidate, the legislative branch of the government is still dominated by the PRI. There are 128 seats in La Cámara de Senadores (the senate), four seats going to each of the thirty-two states, and one of those four is held by whichever party comes in second in that state. Senators also serve six-year terms. La Cámara de Diputados (house of representatives) has five hundred members, who each serve a three-year term.

The Mexican legal system is based on both Spanish civil law and common law, which in its jurisprudence is narrower than in the United States. One of the most powerful juridical instruments is the writ of *amparo* (protection) that can be invoked even against the government. The judicial branch of the government is in its structure very similar to that of the United States, from the Supreme Court down to district courts.

In terms of enforcement of laws and constitutional rights, corruption and *mor-*

GOVERNMENT

didas (bribes) are still rampant throughout the system. Attempts to stop it usually run into the dead end of the underpayment of most government employees. This creates, among other things, a curious symbiosis between the enforcers of the law and those who break it. From traffic fines to privileges in prison, all can be dealt with in money. But petty cash won't do very much once you are in the Reclusorio del Norte (RENO), a huge prison complex on the northern outskirts of Mexico City, nor in the penal colony of Las Islas María, off the coast of Nayarit. The rules are pretty simple: you commit a crime once, you go to prison. A second crime makes you a habitual criminal and you are locked up for twenty years without parole. However, in many provincial prisons detainees are often allowed both to work outside and to have conjugal visits, or even go home. If you should try to run but get caught, there is no law to punish you any further because, legally, no judge could hold it against you that you want to be free.

Bureaucracy, paper shuffling, and the power positions that tenured employees enjoy, can make any *trámite* (formal procedure) lengthy and frustrating. There has been a tremendous effort to tighten up the system, create Web access, and make government user-friendly. New acronyms defining government agencies abound, and here are some essential ones:

CAPUFE	Caminos y Puentes Federales de Ingresos y Servicios Conexos (Federal Roads and Bridges and Linked Services)
CFE	Commisión Federal de Electricidad (Federal Commission for Electricity)
IMSS	Instituto Mexicano del Seguro Social-Solidaridad (Institute of Social Security/Solidarity)
INAH	Instituto Nacional de Antropología e Historia Nacional (Institute of Anthropology and History)
PEMEX	Petróleos Mexicanos (Mexican Petroleum Company)
SEPOMEX	Servicio Postal Mexicano (Mexican Postal Service)
TELMEX	Teléfonos Mexicanos (Mexican Telephone Company)
SEP	Secretaría de Educación Pública (Ministry of Public Education)
UNAM	Universidad Nacional Autónoma de México (National Autonomous University of Mexico)

Related Web links: gob.mx—main access to all government sites (S); inegi.gob.mx—government statistics and acronyms (S); fzln.org.mx/index.php—site of Frente Zapatista de Liberación Nacional (S)

El once negro

The terrorist attack on the *torres gemelos* (twin towers) quickly came to be known as either *el martes negro* (black Tuesday) or *el once negro* (black eleven). Forty-five Latinos died, of whom one-third were Mexican citizens. Although it was suspected that even more undocumented workers died, these rumors could never be confirmed in the painful aftermath of the tragedy.

The immediate response from Latin America, its people and governments, was an overwhelming outpouring of sympathy for the victims, their families, and the United States. As the devastating economic impact on the U.S. service industry from Las Vegas to Atlantic City, with its high numbers of Latino employees, quickly proved, jobs were lost as the number of domestic and foreign tourists diminished considerably.

Further, 9/11 brought the blossoming relationship between the United States. and Mexico to an abrupt halt. The personal friendship between Bush and Fox, the two rookie presidents, was put aside as the focus of international politics shifted to the Middle East. Over time, it cooled off even more with the hesitant reaction of the Mexican government to the U.S. demand for extremely tight border control, and then by the outright opposition of the Mexican government to the war in Iraq.

For its own people, Mexico did make an honest effort to bring the jobless Mexican citizens home and even offered them government work. The response among the Mexican workers in the United States was at best lukewarm, but they eventually regrouped as the economy slowly recovered, and after a year things appeared to be back to pre-9/11 standards.

The deep emotional impact on immigrants as well as the Latino population as a whole has found one compassionate voice in music, the *corridos*. These colorful traditional ballads had just had a powerful comeback with their new controversial topics of illegal immigration and drug trafficking. Since the Mexican Revolution, *corridos* have been reporting in song what is going on in the world, commenting on daily news and recent history. Some well-known groups such as Los Tigres del Norte or the Tucanes de Tijuana, as well as some amateur groups in Los Angeles, picked up on the tragedy in New York. Los Jornaleros del Norte were singing about "el once negro/martes negro" soon after the attack

It remains to be mentioned that one of the heroes after 9/11, Rudy Giuliani, got a vote of confidence from the Mexican capital. So impressed was the local government with his success in dealing with the aftermath in New York City that the mayor of Mexico City hired Mr. Giuliani to come and help fix some of the problems this metropolis faces today.

Related Web links: clubcultura.com/ clubmusica/tigres; lostucanesdetijuana.com— official band sites (E, S)

La Malinche: The Conqueror's Mistress

Behind every great man stands a great woman, they say. Cortés had that woman right by his side: her original Mayan name was Malinali, then Doña Marina after she was baptized; in folk tradition she is called La Malinche. What she accomplished with her language and negotiation skills Cortés and his ruthless soldiers backed up with their swords. So controversial was her role that even after five hundred years her memory lives in infamy. For the Mexican people La Malinche will always be the link between the conquerer and the conquered. She betrayed her own people. She became the "mother" of the mestizos, who since then, and because of her, have been torn between two cultures and two traditions.

Legend describes La Malinche as a beautiful Aztec princess who was taken as a slave by the Mayas to the Yucatán where Cortés found her, freed her, and made her his mistress and most valuable counselor. The truth is somewhat different. According to Bernal Díaz del Castillo, the chronicler of Cortés' expedition, La Malinche was really Mayan and the daughter of a *tlatoani*, lord of a township in Coatzacoalcos on the southern fringes of the Aztec empire. Her mother sold her as a slave and she ended up in a Chontal Mayan village on the Grijalva river, nowadays in the state of Tabasco. In 1519 she was given, along with nineteen other girls, to the Spanish soldiers. Cortés presented her to his friend, Captain Alonso Hernandez Portocarrero.

When Portocarrero returned to Spain, the smart young lady had already shown her translation skills. Growing up with Nahuatl, similar to the language spoken in Tenochtitlán, she had learned Chontal Mayan. Together with Jerónimo de Aguilar, a Spanish missionary who had learned Mayan after he had been shipwrecked, she was able to build the linguistic bridge that was essential for Cortés' ultimate success.

Through her close association with Cortés, La Malinche held a powerful position. She also became his mistress and bore him a son, Martín. History, however, remembers her to this day and age as the original *malinchista*, one who betrays her own people. *Malinchismo* in everyday life, for example, is buying foreign products or *fayuca* (contraband), selling out on traditional values, or crossing over into another culture.

Related Web links: onesun.cc.geneseo.edu/ ~kintz/Malinche.html (E); tihof.org/honors/ malinche.htm (E); hope.edu/latinamerican/ malintzin.html (E); angelfire.com/folk/malinche (S)—accounts of La Malinche

The Luck of the Brave: Cortés and the Gamble of Conquest

When the Spaniards set foot on Hispaniola—what is present-day Haiti and the Dominican Republic—in 1492, nobody along the continental Gulf coast knew about it, and Hernán Cortés was only seven years old. Yucatán, the nearest area on the mainland, was at that time only loosely under the rule of the Aztec empire. The Maya had to pay tribute to Montezuma in the form of goods, slaves, and young braves to still Huitzilopochtli's insatiable thirst for blood and human sacrifice.

Twelve years later Cortés came to the Americas and earned his living as a scribe in Hispaniola and Puerto Rico. Through his participation in the conquest of Cuba he not only earned land but also quickly gained political power. It was there that he first displayed his rare diplomatic skills in a stormy relationship with the governor, his father-in-law.

In terms of romantic relations, his most lasting was no doubt with "Our Lady of Good Luck and Perpetual Coincidence." On his expedition to the mainland with 508 soldiers, sixteen horses, and ten canons he just *happened* to run into two shipwrecked Spaniards near Cozumel who had lived with Mayan tribes for eight years. One of them, Jerónimo de Aguilar, joined their expedition together with some female slaves, among whom happened to be *Malinali*, soon to be baptized Marina. This assertive young lady bridged an important communication gap: she was bilingual in Aztec and Maya. Aguilar, who spoke Maya, could then pass everything on to Cortés in Spanish. Along the whole long Ruta de

Cortés to the final conquest, Malinali operated skillfully as a linguistic and cultural interpreter between the many different people of the Aztec empire and Cortés. In the codices she can be seen next to Cortés, emitting intensive speech bubbles that show her fearlessly negotiating for her master.

On his legendary ascent from the coastal plains of La Villa Rica de la Vera Cruz (now Veracruz), Cortés also *happened* to run into friendly tribes who had grudges against their landlords, the fierce Aztecs: first the Totonacs and then the Tlaxcaltecans, right at the outskirts of the Valley of Mexico, who readily lined up with Cortés' group.

The decisive coincidence, in the end, came from the Aztecs themselves. According to their beliefs, Quetzalcoatl, the feathered serpent god and a savior figure, had predicted his return from the east in the year one reed (by the Aztec calendar). The codices quite precisely described a tall blond man, just like Cortés. Montezuma and his priests were torn between their warrior instincts and their strict obedience to their gods. By the time they saw their mistake, it was too late.

Related Web links: umich.edu/~proflame/texts/ mirror/conflict.html—account of Cortés' life and the conquest (E); fordham.edu/halsall/ mod/aztecs1.html—the Atzec conquest (E)

The Journey of the Aztecs

Nobody will ever know how far north the legendary homeland of the Mexicas extended. It could have been as close as the northern outskirts of present-day Mexico City, or as far as the present-day southwestern United States. The Aztecs' language, Nahuatl, which belongs to the Uto-Aztecan language family, is one of the few clues pointing to the southwestern U.S. location, as the only two other linguistic relatives are the languages of the Pimas and Shoshones.

Oddly enough, we do have the date of their departure (around A.D. 1000) and a—somewhat shrouded—name for this homeland: Aztlán (the place of the heron), also neatly explaining the change from Mexicas to Aztecs. Their arrival in Anáhuac, the Valley of Mexico, is documented in A.D.1325. According to legend, they had to find a place by the water where an eagle sitting on a cactus was devouring a snake. That was the dream of Tenoch, a powerful shaman of their tribe, which determined the place to settle down. And that is where they founded Tenochtitlán, on the shores of Lake Texcoco.

Reality, however, might have looked less heroic. It could have seen a destitute band of ragged and hungry people in desperate search for favorable living conditions. In their long journey south they probably became toughened from deprivation and constant fighting, becoming more aggressive and stronger by making their way in hostile territories. And, still worse, when they finally arrived at the "promised" site, the best land around Lake Texcoco was long taken. So they built their first village on swampy grounds and started to cultivate the marshes.

Within two short centuries they succeeded beyond imagination. From what the surrounding area offered—stone, cedar, oak, and adobe bricks—they built the most incredible city, which they named Tenochtitlán. Located on an island, it was connected by wide causeways to the shore, and fresh water flowed on aqueducts to the island.

Breathtaking temples were built around well-kept plazas to worship a pantheon of gods. Huitzilopochtli, the god of the sun and war, was the most important. To him they had to offer an endless number of human sacrifices. The legendary source of life, the sun, had already been destroyed four times. Only human blood could stop the fifth and final destruction. This constant fear of inevitable doom created an insatiable need for victims, which often came from the Aztecs themselves, but the majority were prisoners of war. This need in turn made the warriors forage more ferociously and range farther abroad, which expanded the boundaries of the powerful empire in a relatively short time.

Related Web links: explora.presidencia.gob.mx/
index_kids.html—history links, not only for kids
(E, S); indians.org/welker/aztec.htm—Aztec
information and links (E)

Dollars and $$

Ferdinand of Aragon and Isabella of Castile sent Columbus "beyond the seas." One of their successors, Charles I, King of Spain, also known as Charles V of the Holy Roman Empire (1516–1556), continued to disregard an age-old warning on the Pillars of Hercules at the western entrance to the Mediterranean: *"ne plus ultra!* (no more beyond)."

With *"plus ultra!* ([go] more beyond)," Charles I offered the perfect challenge to the errant braves of the *reconquista.* When he passed the crown to Philip II in 1556, he truthfully could say, "In my empire the sun never sets." He had watched his men conquer the Americas and the Pacific, including the Philippines—oceans and lands unknown to previous generations.

The royal successors to Charles couldn't always stand their ground in the race for riches by other European powers. Philip V, however, brought the Spanish back on track with his *cedulas reales* (royal decrees) of 1728. Induced by the presence of rich Mexican silver mines, he ordered the minting of a new coin, a silver real worth 8 reales. It showed the Spanish coat of arms with the Latin inscription *"Philip V D G Hispan et Inde* (Philip V, by the grace of God, King of Spain and the Indies)" on one side. On the other stood the Pillars of Hercules entwined with scrolls inscribed with *"plus ultra."* It also displayed the Spanish motto *"VTRAQUE VNVM* (one out of two)." The coin was minted in uniform thickness, silver content, and weight by using screw presses. Quality was assured by appointed assayers, who added their stamp of approval on each coin.

American silver soon financed the whole Spanish Empire. After 1732, the silver real became the most widely accepted coin in the Western Hemisphere. Chinese merchants in the booming tea trade favored it, and it was used all along the many new trails within the rapidly expanding United States. These coins, originally called "pillar dollars," were also known as "pieces of eight" (referring to the 8 reales)—thus the U.S. two bits (25-cent coin) and four bits (50-cent coin) that refer back to the eight sections on the silver real.

It was Jefferson who in 1794 used the $ symbol, derived from the scroll draped around the Pillars of Hercules, for the first U.S. dollars, which had the same weight and silver content as the original 8 reales—27.07 gm, 91.7 percent silver. Mexico uses the same symbol for its peso, but the pillar is represented by a single line only.

Related Web link: coinsite.com/content/faq/
8RealesMilledPillar.asp—facts about early
Spanish coins (E)

77

HISTORY
The Maya

When asked about the presence of the Maya in the Americas, an anthropologist might jokingly respond that when the Spaniards claimed the "new" land, an African, a Chinese man, a Viking, a survivor from Atlantis, and a Martian sat in the bushes along with the Mayan people, all bent over with laughter.

And, on a more serious note, they might continue that hot chocolate was the drink of their high priests, that the natural latex from the sapodilla tree (*achras zapota*) was the original chewing gum, and that popcorn was a Maya invention. While the global context of the original migration of the Native Americans is well researched, the details of the Maya's immediate history are still a mystery.

Even though their power waned a millennium ago, they never quite surrendered. It took the Spaniards only two years to conquer the Valley of Mexico but more than twenty years to subdue the Mayan territories of Yucatán, Guatemala, and Honduras. Ever since the Maya have kept a wary eye on the newcomers. They adapted well and developed their very own survival strategies. Some historians actually see them as the quiet but persistent internal conquistadors.

Few indigenous people apart from the Zapotecs of Oaxaca (led by Benito Juárez) could boast of the likes of a Rigoberta Menchu, winner of the Nobel Peace Prize in 1992, who campaigned for stronger women's rights and worked to raise Mayan consciousness—including thought, language, and pre-Hispanic traditions. Or who could overlook Subcomandante Marcos, a mestizo himself, but one who not only engages in promoting the indigenous cause by force, but faxes his intellectual manifestos out of the jungle of Chiapas, spiked with quotes from Dante, and speaks up for the Mayan and Lacandon peoples?

It is that ongoing adaptation of the Maya to adversity that continues to win them global sympathy. Nowadays the *movimiento Maya* has wholeheartedly embraced computer technology including the World Wide Web. Three thousand years of scientific accomplishments have not disappeared, after all. Obsession with time, space, and building can be witnessed from Tical and Copán to *el caracol* in Chichén Itzá. They celebrated time and space, not only by measuring but rather by applying astronomical knowledge, as can be seen in the stunning displays of light and shadow on the key dates of their astronomical calendar.

The renaissance of the ancient Mayan languages and traditions has lately flourished so abundantly that, good humoredly, it was suggested that Guatemala, home to the majority of Maya people, should be renamed "Guatemaya."

Related Web link: indians.org/welker/maya .htm—comprehensive essay about the Maya (E)

Quetzalcoatl: The Feathered Serpent

Sooner or later every traveler in Mexico will encounter Quetzalcoatl, first just as a name, then as a stone carving or sculpture, or a mythological character playing some part in the conquest. Quetzalcoatl appears in the Aztec legends of creation as god and patron of the priests and healers. As an image and deity he was adopted and made his rounds through all the major Mexican cultures from Teotihuacán to the Aztecs' Tenochtitlán.

In his human shape Quetzalcoatl was said to have been fair-skinned, blond, bearded, and blue-eyed—quite different from the people who surrounded him. Legend praises him as a peace-loving opponent of human sacrifice, which brought about the scorn of the bloodthirsty hierarchy of gods led by the fearsome Xipe Totec, lord of the flayed skin, and the lord-patron of the Mexica, Huitzilopochtli.

Quetzalcoatl was Toltec, the son of Mixcóatl, who founded the city of Tula, just a short way north of Mexico City. At that archaeological site the images of the feathered serpent are numerous. There he ruled until the gods turned against him, weakening his power until he had to leave.

Quetzalcoatl led the Toltecs to the east until they reached the Gulf coast. There he gathered his followers and with a promise that he would one day return, he "fades" away—either sailing, or ascending into the sky and becoming Venus, the morning star. After he was gone, Quetzalcoatl became part of multitribal folklore, spread by the wandering Toltecs. His return was eagerly awaited and even predicted by priests for the year one reed on the Aztec calendar—the same as A.D. 1519. Most of the return theory became true: a blond, blue-eyed man did come sailing in from the east—but it was Cortés. And Montezuma II didn't realize the mistake until it was too late.

Nowadays, one of the most spectacular sites to experience Quetzalcoatl, the feathered serpent god, is in Chichén Itzá in the Yucatán. The Mayas called him Kukulcán, and the builders of *el castillo* (the castle or main pyramid) designed the structure with their astronomers' help so that twice a year, around the spring and fall equinox, Kukulcán comes alive. As the sun goes down, the terraces cast a shadow on the north staircase so that the body of a snake can seem to move. The sculptured head of the snake rests permanently at the pyramid base.

Big crowds gather every spring to see the illusion of the snake undulating down the pyramid to start the cycle of fertility. In fall, the play of light and shadow shows the snake returning to its "den" within *el castillo*.

Quetzalcoatl, Teotihuacán

Permanent Revolution

Cortés, conquistador, set something in motion that is still there: powers vested but not quite accepted; simmering discontent without wanting fundamental change; accepting new ideas while clinging to the old ones.

The indigenous population of Mexico had taken every onslaught on their people and territory with a fatalistic attitude and fought back only when cornered. Consequently, the occupying forces were quickly able to take the land and exploit it the way they knew from their war-torn, recently reconquered Iberian peninsula. From 1522 to the late 1700s, Spain's heavy hand controlled the new territory with ruthless efficiency. They established a "colonial heartland," the area defined by the peripheral points of Veracruz, Oaxaca, Acapulco, Tepic, and San Luis Potosí.

Lack of further conquest to the north brought discontent among the Spaniards and more hardships for the native population, who did not own the land they worked. The Spaniards, both colonizers and military force—¡Viva Mexico! ¡Viva la Independencia!—failed to perceive the cry of the subdued people—¡Muerte a los gachupines! This pent-up frustration finally broke loose with a grito in 1810 by Father Miguel Hidalgo, and sent the country down the path of turmoil and revolution for another hundred years.

In 1822 Agustín de Iturbide, a defected Spanish royalist, declared himself Emperor Agustín I of Mexico. The rebel army of Santa Anna promptly dethroned him in 1823. From then on, Santa Anna managed to hold on to power against Vicente Guerrero and Carlos María de Bustamante, before he was called to the Alamo. In spite of his victory there, Santa Anna could not keep Texas. By 1855 he was replaced by Benito Juárez; shaking off the influence of the Catholic church, he went into exile during the French intervention, only to come back to defeat the French at Querétaro. He executed their established Hapsburg monarch, Maximilian, and then held on to the presidency, on and off, until 1872. Porfirio Díaz, his successor, disregarding the constitutional four-year term for presidents, actually held power for thirty-three years, longer than anybody else, during which time he brought the industrial revolution to Mexico.

By the early 1900s the voices demanding tierra y libertad became louder and louder. Francisco (Pancho) Villa and Emiliano Zapata spread the word, resulting in the bloodiest of all Mexican revolutions. It was not over until 1920, when president Álvaro Obregón called for reconstruction and peace based on the constitution drawn up in 1917. After Obregón was assassinated in 1928, Plutarcho Elías Calles, the elected president, institutionalized revolution by founding the PRI, the Institutional Revolutionary Party!

This party, in spite of its name, was a conservative group that allowed no divergence from its ideology. With an iron grip the party stayed in absolute power until 2000, when the PAN candidate, Vicente Fox, won the presidency. And, to no one's surprise, one of the major issues facing

Presidente Fox has been the uprising of the Zapatistas, a regional indigenous revolution in the south, who once again are demanding *tierra y libertad*.

Related Web links: webdemexico.com.mx/principal/historia.htm—links to Mexican history (S); tamu.edu/ccbn/dewitt/santaanna.htm—Santa Anna (E); historicaltextarchive.com/sections.php?op=viewarticle&artid=336—Porfirio Díaz (E)

Monument to the Niños Héroes, in Chapultepec Park

HOME AND FAMILY
La familia

It is the biological backbone, the spiritual counselor, the formal educator, the financial provider and insurance company, the physical shelter, and the shoulder to cry on: in other words, ¡la familia! The family is the smallest unit in the big puzzle of Mexican life. It can break down to two people, or it can be an intensive network of a spread-out clan. The extended family is a well-functioning hierarchical system of committed individuals based on mutual respect and often valuing others more than themselves.

Workaholic fathers are a minority; if father doesn't show up for dinner, he might be working on his social network, joining his compadres, his "co-fathers"—ties that go beyond family and run deeply, widely across society without consideration of socioeconomic levels. Compadres are often the godfathers of a friend's child. Should anything happen to the father and mother, the compadre's family will take in the orphaned child and provide for everything.

Another reason for father not to join his family at night is a relationship called *casa chica*, where he maintains another household with a mistress and their children. This is often tolerated by the wife because it is somewhat of a continuation of pre-marital behavior. Back then, the *novio* (boyfriend, fiancé) could experience freely, while *la prometida* (fiancée), was carefully kept away from anyone (including her boyfriend) who could threaten her virginity. It is a "boys will be boys" attitude with all its sexual and societal ramifications.

Finally, father arrives home for *la cena* (dinner). As the head of the family, he will be in charge. As a macho, he believes in the role that fate prescribed for him. He is the authority, and tries to do his best. He loves and dotes on his children, serves as a role model when he represents the family in society, and has his wife on a pedestal.

And this is as well as the system can work, anticipating disagreement and accepting it as long as personal dignity and honor are not questioned. After all, the father is not the only one calling the shots. His parents might still be around to tell him what to do. In other words, it is formality rather than reasoning that makes survival of the family structure possible. It is a matter of accepting your role and living with it:

El padre de familia is in charge of the family, their well-being, education, and respect. He has great responsibilities and enjoys personal freedom.

La madre takes care of the children and the household, which includes maids, meals, hosting parties, and shining at social occasions. Her ideas, when sanctioned by the hierarchy above, turn into reality.

El hijo (the son) tries to retain his father's approval while being emotionally attached to his mother.

La hija (the daughter), emotionally guided by her mother, has to learn the intricate patterns and clandestine ways of the woman to be able to survive in society.

La tía (the aunt), an unmarried relative, takes over part of the household chores to earn her stay. She is often a chaperone to dating children, often an "invisible angel," absorbing and buffering the bigger shocks in domestic relationships.

La empleada, la muchacha (the maid), is everyone's confidante. She reigns in the kitchen, hears all the stories, listens, and smiles. She knows what is going on, and sometimes picks a favorite cause and makes it, quietly, happen.

El ahijoado, la ahijada (the godchild) was in need of shelter and is taken in because of *el compadrazgo* (this relationship). The godchildren fit in wherever they can and help out, but lead a Cinderella-type existence.

Los abuelos (grandparents) are revered by everybody and half listened to, but wield an uncontested authority when it matters.

Y los demas parientes (and all the other relatives) might live in the household and do their part to make the extended family living situation work.

All these components would spell disaster in many other environments, but in Mexico it may spark spontaneous fiestas, with the godchild putting on outrageous music, grandsons dancing with their spinster aunts, granddaughters joking with their grandfathers, and mothers flirting with their husbands.

The Cathedral of Mexico City

Machismo: I'm the King

El machismo is something *muy mexicano* (very Mexican) and has many faces. It is, naturally, all about men. In other cultures manliness often only covers one side of a man: toughness, strength, probably being a jock, and the desire to show off, but rarely showing emotions. In Mexico it includes, when deemed necessary, uncompromising aggression toward other men as well as vulnerability, rejection, and an ambivalent stance toward women—on one hand cocky, assertive, and relentlessly aggressive, on the other often spitefully subordinate, even shriveling before an idolized mother figure, or bursting into uncontrollable fits of anger. When honor is at stake nobody should doubt the man's virility or slander his wife and family.

It is a difficult role to play. For those machos who succeed, a popular singer and composer, José Alfredo Jiménez, has just the right song: "El rey (The King)," which can be heard throughout Mexican *cantinas* and *pulquerías* (bars). It is widely considered *the* macho anthem.

It is about crying into *una copa de Tequilai* while trying to come to terms with lost love. It's an emotional mixture of the macho's own misery combined with his commiseration with the evil woman who abandoned him and will now live to regret it. She will also lie about her true feelings, which she will have to hide forever.

If any honor is saved in such a situation it comes from self-persuasion: rejection will hurt the one who inflicted it even more. And, at the same time, aren't there many other conquests to be made? It is essential to take advantage of every opportunity. And some men do just that with a vengeance: *"Pues, ¡yo soy el mero, mero!* (After all, I'm the one and only!)" But the song continues to explain. After the initial bout of self-pity and, most likely, *una cruda tremenda*, (a horrible hangover) a real macho gets up and remembers that he is, after all, still *el rey* (the king), one who will do whatever he wants. No one really can understand him even though his word is always *la ley* (the law).

Of course not all Mexican men strike that pose, but what they saw and heard in their formative years probably encouraged some degree of *machismo*: a mother who rules the house while father is frequently gone (perhaps to a mistress in *una casa chica*); and in the meanwhile the mother lavishes her love on her children, idolizes her sons, and instills father's "virtues" in them. This pattern has been repeated for generations throughout a violent past. Today's macho attitudes and fatalism go back long before the conquest of 1521 to the Aztec warrior society as well as to the medieval Spanish knight's honor codes.

Changing social attitudes, education, and a growing emancipation of women all over Latin America will eventually dismantle the traditional roles. Growing divorce rates now offer more women an escape from extreme macho behavior or the sometimes resulting abuses, while a die-hard macho can't quite play out his usual range of macho games anymore.

Related Web link: elmariachi.com/songs/ el_rey.asp—lyrics of the song *El Rey* by José Alfredo Jiménez (E, S)

Life Cycle

National health care provides good pre-natal support as well as delivery facilities in many areas. Rural clinics are limited in their possibilities but can be called on in case of emergencies. In the more remote areas, *parteras* (midwifes) assist at the birth, while further advice to the mother is often given by local *farmacias* (drugstores), and still frequently from *curanderos*. Infant mortality is still rather high: 26 per 1,000 live births, as compared to 7 in the United States (but 37 just across the border in Guatemala).

The life cycle revolves around the many traditions grounded in the Catholic religion. Ninety percent of the population adhere to Catholicism: if not always spiritually, they at least observe the more folkloric aspects of their religion. Although church and state have been strictly separated since the mid 1800s, when convents had to be abandoned and religious attire was banned in public, open religious celebrations have made their way back into society through colorful processions and exhibitions during major events of the church year. Observers of the yearly religious cycle will not miss any of the following:

January 1	*Año Nuevo* (New Year's Day)
January 6	*Los Santos Reyes* (Epiphany)
January 17	San Antonio Abád (Saint Anthony, Abbot) for animal blessings
February 2	Virgen de la Candelaria (Candlemas), a fiesta
February 3	San Blas (St. Blaise), blessing against any throat pains
February 14	San Valentín, day of love and friendship
moveable feasts	*El Miércoles de Ceniza* (Ash Wednesday), beginning of Lent, *El Domingo de Ramos* (Palm Sunday), the beginning of *la Semana Santa* (Holy Week), including Good Friday, Easter Saturday, and Easter Sunday
May/June	*La Ascensión* (Ascension Day), *Pentecostés* (Whitsun)
June	Corpus Christi
August	*La Transfiguración de Jesucristo* (Transfiguration)
November 1	*Todos los Santos* (All Saints' Day)
November 2	*El día de los muertos* (Day of the Dead, All Souls' Day)
December 8	*La Inmaculada Concepción* (Immaculate Conception)
December 12	Nuestra Señora de Guadalupe, patron saint of Mexico
December 16–24	*Las posadas*, looking for shelter nine days before Christmas
December 24	*Noche Buena* (Christmas Eve)
December 25	*Navidad* (Christmas Day)

December 28 Los Santos Inocentes
(Holy Innocents),
celebrated like April
Fools' Day

December 31 San Silvestre (New Year's
Eve)

On any day of the year personal saints and name givers, as well as patron saints of churches and communities are celebrated. For example, any boy named Tomás can have a celebration on July 3, marked on the calendar for San Tomás Apóstol. A church dedicated to Santiago (St. James) will have a feria on July 25, and the whole city of San Antonio could celebrate January 17.

Of course there are also many public festivities throughout the year:

February 5 Proclamación de la
Constitución de 1917
(Constitution Day)

February 24 El día de la bandera
(Flag Day)

March 18 Expropiación petrolera
(nationalization of oil
industry, 1938)

March 21 Birthday of President
Benito Juárez (1806–
1872)

April 14 El día de las Américas

April 30 El día del niño
(Children's Day)

May 1 El día del trabajo (Labor
Day)

May 5 Cinco de Mayo,
commemorating the
battle of Puebla (1862)

May 10 El día de las madres
(Mother's Day)

May 15 El día del maestro
(Teachers' Day)

June El día del padre (Father's
Day), celebrated on the
second Sunday

September 16 El día de la independencia

October 12 El día de la raza
(Columbus Day)

November 20 Aniversario de la
revolución mexicana

Personal landmarks are celebrated in the journey from birth to death, interspersed within this yearly cycle. El bautizo (baptism) makes the newborn a member of the church, as well as giving him/her the first social ties through padrinos and madrinas (godfather and godmother).

School attendance starts at the age of six. La confirmación (confirmation) between ages ten and fourteen makes the child's ties to the church even stronger, combined with frequent confessions (nowadays "reconciliation") and taking of the Host. Girls often go through an elaborate quinceañera for their fifteenth birthday, a celebration that sometimes rivals a wedding in pomp and expenses. After age fifteen many children join the workforce while others get their bachillerato. Before marriage, a couple goes through an extended noviazgo (engagement), although the poor can enter a common-law union without great circumstance. Formal weddings tend to be very similar to other countries as many U.S. customs have been adopted. Church ceremonies are a must, since el santo matri-

monio (holy matrimony) is one of the sacraments.

Official divorce rates are extremely low (4 percent of all registered marriages, compared to 49 percent in the United States), but many couples live unofficially separated. It is no longer true that while women and mothers stay at home, men work. More and more, women need to earn money to contribute to a better lifestyle. *La jubilación* (retirement) is more accessible in government jobs than for rural workers and owners of small businesses. The latter usually pass ownership on to their immediate family and keep a senior position with a reduced workload.

Some *ancianos* (the old) rise to a respected position in their barrio or town. They'll know if they succeeded if everyone starts addressing them reverently, adding "don" or "doña" to their name and seeking out their advice.

For Mexicans death is viewed as the final step of life. *El velatorio* (the wake) brings the family and friends together over food and drink, accompanied by singing, long prayers, and the visitors' expressing their *pésame* (condolences). This is followed by a last visit to church in a *funeral solemne*, with the number of people attending indicating the deceased person's status. The following nine days (*la novena*) helps the mourners to better cope with their loss. Widowers return to normal life fairly quickly, and often remarry, while widows tend to wear black the rest of their lives and enjoy a special status in the community, polishing their deceased husband's image into a quasi-sainthood that benevolently reflects back on them.

Related Web links: catholic-forum.com/saints/ indexsnt.htm—index of patron saints (E); vivasancarlos.com/Calendar.html—calendar of Mexican fiestas (E)

Teenagers and the Dating Game

In dating part of the fun is to overcome obstacles. This used to be played out secretly, behind the careful watch of parental eyes, or blatantly in public meeting places, mostly the zocalos all over the country.

There are benches all around the square, and a *quiosco* in the center provides an elevated platform for occasional musicians or for the guys to hang out. Should a group of girls appear and start around the plaza clockwise, the boys get up and pass them twice each round, in the opposite direction. Any eye contact lingering long enough is all a young man needs for encouragement to get his network going. Friends of friends and relatives are diplomatically deployed to initiate communication between the would-be lovers.

The girl might agree to a chaperone scam, going to a movie supervised by a sister who also has clandestine plans; they leave the house together, meet their dates, and return at an agreed-on hour to walk home together giggling and chatting about a movie they never got to see.

The boy, on the other hand, might gather up his courage after that promising glance in the plaza and plan a serenade at the girl's window. A solo performance of a romantic bolero could work, but most *enamorados* (those in love) summon up their friends or a group of mariachis to impress the lady. Now, she can either acceptingly catch the bouquet of flowers the pretender tosses up to the balcony, or refuse, take her chamber pot, and empty it over the unfortunate suitor.

Just like chamber pots, these scenes are mostly a thing of the past. The zocalo, however, remains an important place for social encounters. Cruising around the square by car has become an impressive alternative, in addition to *discotecas* and *bailes* (dances), while etiquette still obliges parents to send along chaperones who are to guard their daughters' innocence. Only in the bigger cities or more liberal and intellectual circles have women been able to assert themselves as guardians of their own moral welfare. Society as a whole still frowns on aggressive female behavior promoting emancipation in spite of women taking on more and more responsibilities outside the house.

Within the last generation, the dating scene has changed radically. Technology and the number of other entertainment options available for *enamorados* to get close to "the one and only" have exploded. Unnoticed, however, by the traditions governing that complicated mating dance of *el macho*, the "he," and *la hembra*, the "she," the baselines have stayed the same. He often will formally court his *novia* jealously, guarding and defending her honor and virginity while at the same time relentlessly chasing and conquering any skirt in sight, using the *discoteca*, the phone, or the Internet.

As always and anywhere, true love will often cut right through all parental expectations and societal demands, as it did throughout history. After all, Cortés found La Malinche and Frida Kahlo found Diego Rivera, twice.

Sundays at Chapultepec Park

One of the best places to observe, even participate in, the magic feeling of spontaneous fiesta is on Sundays in Chapultepec Park in Mexico City. After morning mass, busses, subways, *colectivos* (see page 142), and taxis unload hundreds of families carrying big bulging bags with all the makings for a country picnic. Everybody, from babies to great-grandmothers, including spinster aunts, compadres and their families, friends, and, often, *unos perritos* (puppies) all hurry to claim a spot on the grassy grounds in the shade of the tall eucalyptus trees. Their excitement is tangible and there is much ado about getting settled.

Blankets, chairs, snacks, and drinks come out as vendors descend on the picnickers. If there is a birthday to be celebrated, a piñata can be bought, clowns hired, and food supplies easily replenished. Traditional delicacies abound from tamales, tacos, *pancita* (tripe stew), jicama with lime and hot sauce, *chicharrones* (fried pork rinds), nuts and seeds, lollipops, *aguas* (flavored water) and *refrescos* (sodas), and *raspadas* (frosties), churros, corn on the cob, and peeled and ready-to-eat mangos on a stick next to appetizing plates of freshly cut fruit.

Most of the visitors, however, come well prepared with their own food. They will set up their own little barbecue, volleyball nets, a piñata, or even a portable TV so the men can watch a Sunday afternoon soccer match. The women hover over the food and the children run around chasing their dog or kicking a soccer ball.

Once the picnic is ready, the families settle down on their blankets. Strolling musicians might stop by while they enjoy their food. Passing vendors are often lucky by tapping into the happy and carefree *ambiente* of the afternoon, selling *tiliches* (knickknacks) such as balloons, wind wheels, *papalotes* (kites), and so on. Sundays in Chapultepec are like country fairs.

Once the meal is over and a little siesta taken, there are other opportunities to be explored. *Los jóvenes* (teenagers) might sneak away from the watchful eyes of their parents to *agarrar la onda* (catch what's happening), find some *chicas*, and invite them for a quick row around the small lake, visit the zoo, climb up to the National History Museum in Chapultepec Castle, or just cross La Reforma to marvel at the Museo Nacional de Antropología, which might just on that particular Sunday have the *voladores of Papantla* (the flying men from Papantla, Veracruz) perform their awesome ceremony.

Tlaloc, god of rain and storm, in front of the National Museum of Anthropology in Mexico City

The Volcanoes: Legends, Fire, and Snow

On the eastern rim of the Valle de Anáhuac (Valley of Mexico) loom the two snow-covered peaks of Popocatépetl to the right and Iztaccíhuatl to the left. It's the combination of these two shapes that has inspired the imagination of ancient story-tellers as well as more recent poets and writers. An Aztec legend, however, tells the most popular version frequently seen in paintings on Mexican calendars.

The story says that in the beginning of time when the mountains hadn't taken their final forms yet, the Mexicas (Aztecs) arrived on the shores of Texcoco to build the city of Tenochtitlán.

It was soon thereafter that a princess named Mixtli was born to Tizoc, the great Tlatoani (emperor) of the Aztecs. Mixtli turned into a most beautiful princess. Many young noblemen fell under her spell, especially Axooxco, a very short-tempered, violent warrior, who was the most persistent. Mixtli, however, rejected his advances because her heart already belonged to Popoaca, a commoner who could only dispute Axooxco's demands if he proved himself in battle and would gain the status of "Knight of the Eagle."

As Mixtli saw him leave for the battle-fields she despaired over her own love and the unsurmountable dangers Popoaca had to face. Malicious rumors spread by Axooxco increased Mixtli's anxieties so much that she took her own life. But then Popoaca returned in triumph as a celebrated Eagle Warrior. Seeing his love dead he took her body toward the mountains. There he sat down, bent over her lifeless shape and hop-ing that the cold winds and snow would

eventually wake her up. It is since then that Popocatépetl (Smoking Mountain) is wait-ing for the day he'll be able to take Iztac-cíhuatl (Sleeping Woman) home.

These days people swear that Popo's patience is finally running out. He has been fuming with such violent eruptions that the immediate surrounding areas have frequently been put on red alert.

While, therefore, Popo has been off limits for mountain climbers, Ixta is still slumbering peacefully. With an altitude of 17,342 ft she is slightly lower than Popo (17,887 ft), but with the rugged access still presents an equally formidable challenge to the mountaineer.

From the Paso de Cortés (12,045 ft), between Popo and Ixta, which Hernán Cortés crossed on his epic journey from Veracruz to Tenochtitlán in 1519, three other volcanic destinations in the volcano belt lure the prospective climber from a distance. To the east, just beyond the city of Puebla stands Matlalcueyatl or "La Mal-inche" (13,383 ft), dwarfed by the Pico de Orizaba or Citlaltépetl (18,516 ft) in the far background. On a clear day, to the west, the Nevado de Toluca or Xinantécatl (15,124 ft) sends a snowy invitation to pro-spective cross-country skiers between November and March.

And far beyond what the eye can see, west toward the Pacific Ocean, there are many more of those sleeping and recently very active volcanoes. One is the Volcano de Fuego in the state of Colima, not far from the volcano of Paricutín (Michoacán), which erupted and buried the village of San Juan with lava and ash on February 23, 1943.

Buried church of Paricutín, Michoacán

Related Web links: volcano.und.nodak.edu—
volcano activity and country profiles (E);
volcano.und.nodak.edu/vwdocs/volc_images/
img_paricutin.html—photos of Paricutín (E)

The Regions of Mexico

Cortés, asked by King Charles V to tell him what Mexico looked like, took a piece of paper, crumpled it up, and held it out on his flat hand. Mexico from high above looks indeed as if it has been involved in a tug-of-war between the lush tropical south and the northern deserts across the line of the Tropic of Cancer, bunching up the land to mountains, the "V" shape of the Sierra Madre Occidental and the Sierra Madre Oriental that meet in La Junta, a twisted knot south of Mexico City. This tremendous upheaval continues on as Sierra Madre del Sur to Chiapas. Volcanoes form a belt across the center of the country from east to west, reaching the highest altitude of Mexico, and third highest of North America, in Citlaltépetl, probably better known as Pico de Orizaba.

Between the "V" lie the heartlands of Mexico, the Valle de Anáhuac with cosmopolitan Mexico D.F. (Federal District of Mexico City) and the altiplano (highlands) of the north occupying about half the Mexican territory.

From Chiapas in the south, a sweep to the northeast takes us to the brush-covered, rather flat peninsula of the Maya, Yucatán. The coastline with an abundance of beaches, more than in any other country of the Americas south of the U.S. border, completes the picture. The following is but one of many ways to categorize the regions of Mexico:

1. Dry Baja California, the longest peninsula in the world; favorite destination for U.S. fishermen, whale watchers, off-road enthusiasts, and the beach crowd.
2. The "Mexican Riviera": the Pacific coast from Guaymas to Salina Cruz, and including the resort towns of Mazatlán, Puerto Vallarta, Manzanillo, Zihuatanejo, Acapulco, Puerto Escondido, and others.
3. The altiplano: the highlands, between the Sierra Madre chains from Chihuahua, the Copper Canyon, Guadalajara, more colonial cities, archaeological sites in Tula, Teotihuacán, and the extended metropolitan area of Mexico City down to Oaxaca.
4. The Gulf Coast and Huasteca: the eastern slope of the Sierra Madre Oriental attracts much domestic tourism but also includes the pyramids in Tajin, Zempoala, Palenque, and the beaches along the Gulf Coast.
5. The Yucatán peninsula: prime maritime resorts in Isla Mujeres, Cancún, and the Maya sites of Chichén Itzá, Uxmal, and Tulúm.
6. The highlands of Chiapas: land of Lacandon and Chamula Indians, colorful indigenous markets, San Cristóbal de Las Casas and a thriving modern capital, Tuxtla Gutiérrez.

The thirty-two political regions

STATE NAME	OFFICIAL ABBREVIATION
Aguascalientes	AGS
Baja California	BC

Baja California Sur	BCS	Oaxaca	OAX
Campeche	CAM	Puebla	PUE
Chiapas	CHIS	Querétaro	QRO
Chihuahua	CHIH	Quintana Roo	QROO
Coahuila	COAH	San Luis Potosí	SLP
Colima	COL	Sinaloa	SIN
Distrito Federal	DF	Sonora	SON
Durango	DGO	Tabasco	TAB
Guanajuato	GTO	Tamaulipas	TAMPS
Guerrero	GRO	Tlaxcala	TLAX
Hidalgo	HGO	Veracruz	VER
Jalisco	JAL	Yucatán	YUC
México	MEX	Zacatecas	ZAC
Michoacán	MICH		
Morelos	MOR		
Nayarít	NAY		
Nuevo León	NL		

Related Web link: www.visitmexico.com—
Mexican tourism site (E, S)

La Junta (the knot), the southern end of the Sierras

Mexico, México, and ¡México!: All Good Things Come in Threes

"**C**omo México no hay dos (There's only one Mexico)" goes the saying, exulting and condemning what the citizens hate to love and love to hate. It's a popular line in mariachi songs that without fail brings tears to the eyes of most Mexicans abroad. But contrary to that saying, there are actually three Mexicos.

First and above all there is *la República*, the federal republic with its 100,294,036 inhabitants (as estimated in July 1999) occupying 1,972,550 km² of North America. The official name is Los Estados Unidos Mexicanos, with a centralized government, thirty-one states, and one federal district.

The second México is *el estado de México* (the state of Mexico), which almost entirely surrounds Mexico City. Its capital city is Toluca, some forty-fve miles west of Mexico City. It lies at the highest altitude of any state in the country and attracts local tourists, mainly from Mexico City, with its pine forests, blue lakes (Valle de Bravo), archaeological sites (Teotihuacán, Malinalco), National Parks (Nevado de Toluca, Desierto de los Leones), spas (Ixtapan de la Sal), a popular pilgrimage shrine (Chalma), and weekend playgrounds such as La Marquesa on Highway 15 about half way between Mexico City and Toluca.

The third Mexico is commonly referred to as "D.F." for *Distrito Federal*. It comprises Mexico City and its immediate surrounding area in the Valle de Anáhuac (Valley of Mexico), the great basin between the southern end of the two Sierra Madre ranges. For lack of opportunity else-

where in the country this cosmopolitan area has drawn multitudes of destitute people since pre-Columbian times. In the 1400s, as Tenochtitlán, the capital of the Aztec empire, it far surpassed the medieval cities of Europe in population and infrastructure. Today failure of agrarian reform and distribution of the land throughout *la República* has maintained a steady flow of people from the country to the city. By the end of the second millennium, this movement had created the biggest urban area in the world. By now, twenty million call the D.F. their home, and the predicted growth should take this number to twenty-six million people by 2020.

Related Web links: mexicocity.gob.mx—Ministry of Tourism (E, S); **edomexico.gob.mx**—state of Mexico (S); **mexico.udg.mx**—broad website on Mexico from University of Guadalajara (S)

The Climate . . . and What to Do About It

Every possible climate on earth is represented somewhere in Mexico at some time during the year. The zones, often mere pockets or strata of micro climates, depend on the altitude and change between the dry season (October to May) and the rainy season (June to September). The Tropic of Cancer cuts across the country slightly north of Tampico to Mazatlán and the southern tip of Baja California, which puts about the southern two-thirds of Mexico into the torrid zone. May and early June are the hottest months, especially in the coastal lowlands, when frequent rainfalls add uncomfortable humidity.

Visitors should be aware of the crucial 27°C (80°F) threshold that controls a tourist's comfort zone. Below that, nights get cool and clammy. Too much above means tropical heat, which keeps everybody sweating and mosquitoes and other insects awake. That threshold often lies between *la tierra caliente*, the coastal lowlands, and *la tierra fría*, the mountains and high plateaus. Just driving inland for an hour or two will quickly dry off the sweat and eventually bring out the need for sweaters.

Based on climate charts, a tourist can make many choices, first the season and then the altitude of the destination. The climate also controls hotel prices, which depend on the time of the year and, of course, the number of tourists. The beaches south of Mazatlán tend to be sweltering hot in the summer months whereas the central highlands are usually pleasant with regular afternoon showers or sometimes torrential *chubascos* (rainstorms).

Observing the locals will give the traveler the best clue on what to wear and do to promote overall comfort. After all, regional culture, architecture, and traditions (e.g., the siesta), as well as a noticeable variety of *trajes típicos regionales* (regional clothing styles) have been largely determined by the weather.

White, airy *manta* (cotton fabric), bought in the market by the meter, has been the favorite material for long pants, shirts, blouses, and skirts worn by the rural indigenous population in the hotter regions. *Chamarras* (thick woolen jackets) and heavy serapes (ponchos) keep men warm in the colder climate while women wrap up in the versatile *rebozo* (extra large shawl).

Progress has of course made synthetic clothes readily and cheaply available in every market in the country. Typical clothing is, actually, receding more and more into the less accessible areas or is only brought out for fiestas and performances for tourists.

City folks dress like the rest of the Western world—except that middle- and upper-class men like to wear a guayabera (a lose, pleated shirt), perfect for tropical climates and any social occasion. And should they be surprised by a sudden *aguacero* (cloudburst) they might, just like country folk, improvise with a huge banana leaf for a make-shift poncho.

Related Web links: clima.terra.com— weather forecast (S); smn.cna.gob.mx—national meteorological service (S)

Names and Nicknames

El día del santo (a person's saint's day) and birthday were, and still sometimes are, one and the same. Catholic tradition tended to encourage parents to give the newborn the saint's name on the calendar. Therefore, on February 14 a child would be christened Valentino or Valentina, whereas Patricio or Patricia were probably born on March 17 (St. Patrick's Day) and June 29 gave parents the choice between Pedro, Pablo, or Paulina as this day was dedicated to the two major apostles, St. Peter and St. Paul.

The ever popular birthday song, "Las mañanitas," confirms that very tradition in its first lines:

Estas son las	These are the
mañanitas	morning songs
que cantaba el	which King David
rey David,	used to sing
en el día de	on your saint's
tu santo,	(= birth) day,
te las cantamos	and we sing it this
así:	way:
Despierta, mi	Wake up, my dear,
bien despierta...	wake up . . .

Nowadays this tradition is no longer the rule. Although Catholic names are still most prevalent, some foreign names (e.g., Jennifer, Sandra, Rita) are very popular, as are some old Aztec names that show a sense of patriotism (e.g., Xochi [flower], Cuitlahuac [a famous Aztec leader]).

But no matter which name is given, *apodos* (nicknames) are common. José becomes Pepe, Ignacio is shortened to Nacho, as are Roberto (Beto), Francisco (Pancho), Guadalupe (Lupe), Jesús (Chucho), Concepción (Concha), and Enrique (Quique).

Often physical characteristics or shortcomings label people in a surprisingly accepted way. Protruding eyes will bring about Sapo (toad), or a person with a flat nose might end up with the nickname Chato (pugnose). "Un güero" might be a gringo or just a blond-haired guy. "Nacos" are country pumpkins, probably a degrading ethnic reference to the Totonac people of Veracruz.

All Veracruzanos are, in turn, subject to be labeled "jarochos," residents of Mexico City are "chilangos," the Guadalajara area is populated by "tapatios," and Yucatán is full of "Yucas."

In official *trámites* (legal procedures), everybody needs to be identified with given name(s): father's last name and mother's maiden name, for example, María Sánchez Bareña. Middle initials are not used, but the first name might consist of a string of names. The principle saints' names are often narrowed down to very specific ones: Teresita de Jesus or Teresa de Avila, María del Pilar, María Dolores, María Magdalena, María de la Luz, María Guadalupe, or María Concepcion. Often, María is "understood" and the girls are simply called Pilar, Dolores, or Luz.

Now, if María Sánchez Bareña marries Luis Paredes Ruiz, she will be known as María Sánchez de Paredes. Her children might be Francisco Paredes Sánchez and Araceli Paredes Sánchez. Bareña and Ruiz, the parents' mothers' maiden names, have disappeared.

Transportation

There are many ways to get around and for any budget and social class. In fact, the old system of first-, second-, third-, and probably fourth-class travel seems to be well and alive in Mexico. This doesn't necessarily mean categorizing the population or segregating people to designated areas in planes, buses, or trains, but rather looking at the service according to remoteness of the destination and the condition of the roads or landing facilities.

The major airlines—Aeromexico, Mexicana de Aviación, and others—take care of international flights and go domestically to wherever their modern fleet can land. That might be limited to the 230 or more airports with paved runways. The 1,500 unpaved airstrips are used by military and government planes as well as numerous charter companies, air taxis, and private planes. Apparently, demand has also kept older models flying way beyond their life expectancy. It's entirely possible to enjoy a nostalgic flight in a vintage DC-3.

Travelers who'd rather stay on the road have many choices. Super modern luxury buses (de lujo) roaring down the *autopistas* (freeways), often *cuotas* (toll roads), offer comfortable reclining seats, video programs, air conditioning, clean restrooms, and smiling attendants. *Primera clase* (first-class buses) also have numbered seats and most of the above amenities. *Segunda clase* (second class) is slower, stops often on demand along the route, and may be crowded, including the infamous chickens and pigs, to a point of standing room only. Still cheaper are privately

owned *camionetas* (trucks), that have passengers standing up in the back. They sometimes operate parallel to the faster lines but frequently depart from the final destination of *la segunda*.

Thanks to the efficient buses and ever-improving road system, train travel has been steadily declining. The government-run Ferrocarriles Nacionales de México (FNM, Mexican National Railroads) is apparently gone for good, and its once bustling hub, Buena Vista station in Mexico City, is shut down. A private company, Ferrocarril Mexicano (Ferromex) now handles mostly freight and is well connected to the U.S. railroads (Nafta Trains). While regular passenger service is entirely relegated to the bus lines, Ferromex has revamped the popular tourist route through the Copper Canyon and come up with other ideas. Their Tequila Express, for example, takes tourists on a round-trip from Guadalajara to the town of Tequila and, at the same time, on a culinary, musical (mariachis), and folkloric immersion into the traditions of Tequila.

Another plan is still in the works: the Maya Express, a tourist train running 342 miles (570 km), five-day tours from Chichén Itzá to Palenque with stopovers in Mérida and Campeche, highlighting archaeology as well as the Yucatán cuisine and its history and regional customs.

Related Web links: ferromex.com.mx—private railway company website (S); aeromexico.com, mexicana.com.mx—airline websites (E, S)

A Babel of Languages: To Save or Not to Save?

As Mexico has moved up to be the biggest Spanish-speaking country in the world, it has neglected its more than sixty indigenous languages. Mainstream culture has readily incorporated words from many languages into its vocabulary, but all those other living languages of the indigenous peoples are often degradingly referred to as *dialectos* (dialects).

A group of about fifty people, under the umbrella of La Casa de los Escritores en Lenguas Indigenas (home of writers in indigenous languages) is trying to give these languages official, even constitutional, acknowledgment and equality with the predominant *castellano*, or Spanish. Bowing to Indian literary tradition from Nezahualcóyotl to current writers, they emphasize the prolific use of Indian words in the Mexican language. From *ahuacatl* (avocado), *chocolatl* (chocolate), and *tomatl* (tomato), the Nahuatl language and culture proves that it has delivered enough goods and terminology to deserve recognition. In addition, 2.5 million Aztec survivors still uphold the Nahuatl language and oral tradition.

But it is not only official and outside recognition that are needed. The speakers of all these indigenous languages themselves have to surmount the inferior status accorded most aspects of their living culture. They suffer from the contradiction inherent in seeing their ancestors being exalted in museums on one hand, while on the other thoughtless discrimination abounds in the current national scheme.

Although legally mandated, bilingual education is failing miserably, not for lack of want but for practical restrictions. There are neither enough qualified teachers nor enough language programs at the college level. Not even UNAM, the university in Mexico City and the oldest in the Americas, has a full-fledged department of indigenous languages.

This group of indigenous writers is working on solutions by developing materials and methods to make the Indians literate in their own language, but teachers are hard to find. They realize it's not enough to speak a language to know how to teach it, and it is even harder to convince the Indians to preserve what had always proved a hindrance for them.

The top ten indigenous languages

RANK	LANGUAGE	NUMBER OF SPEAKERS
1.	Nahuatl (Aztec)	2.5 million
2.	Maya	1.5 million
3.	Zapotec	800,000
4.	Mixtec	770,000
5.	Otomí	560,000
6.	Tzotzil	520,000
7.	Purépecha	200,000
8.	Tarahumara	120,000
9.	Totonac	100,000
10.	Popolac	30,000

Related Web links: indigena.org/e-indigenas .html—links for the 56 indigenous peoples of Mexico (E); zompist.com/indianwd.html— Nahuatl word lists (E); ethnologue.com/show _country.asp?name=Mexico—listing of 288 languages spoken in Mexico (E)

Spanglish, or Is It Espanglés?

From the very beginning, encounters between the Spanish and other settlers along *la frontera* (the border), have sparked a spontaneous linguistic reaction, one that continues to simmer. The political border today, clearly defined and guarded as it is, does not quite allow a merging of the Germanic and Romance language families, as happened in Britain after 1066. But constant linguistic intrusions across those political and cultural lines has forced adjustments to both English and Spanish to facilitate communication. The result is what is widely called Spanglish. Words, structures, and concepts are taken into the other language, where they are bent and twisted to fit into syntax, lexicon, and cultural content.

This means functioning in a society with a long history of moving back and forth between two cultures. Cultural tagging—that is, naming things from the other culture with its linguistically adjusted word—occurs anywhere two languages meet so intimately. "A truck" can become *una troca*, "to weld" turns into *belder/velder/guelder*, and a "home run" might show up as *jonron* in the local newspaper.

Spanglish has definitely grown into a vehicle for easy communication and is here to stay. It convincingly reflects the massive presence of Spanish-speaking immigrants as well as the influence of the U.S. economy on the rest of the world.

On both sides there are educated purists who regard mixing languages as an abomination. At first glance Spanglish actually might look like a gibberish hodgepodge of randomly selected words, phrases, sentences from both languages, or the inability to stay within one. At a closer look, however, one can soon distinguish some basic, but not necessarily restrictive, rules:

1. Replacing individual words ("*Dame five*" from "Give me five").
2. Spanishize/anglicize (*chequear el aceite*, from "check the oil"; *mesteña* from "mustang").
3. Switching back and forth whole structures that should flow without interfering with the syntax of either language ("*Ayer mi abuela and I fuimos al mall para ver las ofertas de Thanksgiving*").
4. Longer sequences of speech (while speaking in English a thrown-in Spanish word might trigger a switch to Spanish altogether, or vice versa).

These rules have been mastered best by the people who actually live and breathe the two cultures on a daily basis. Spanglish is increasingly used by radio announcers, performing artists, writers, and poets. This so-called code switching automatically expands the communication horizon to express and understand references from two language traditions. This means accessing two huge cultural reservoirs that rank among the top five most widely spoken languages in the world.

Related Web links: chronicle.com/free/v47/i07/07b00701.htm—a comprehensive paper on the gravitas of Spanglish (E); members.tripod.com/~nelson_g/spanglish.html— a Spanglish dictionary (S)

Buckaroos, Vaqueros, *Charros*: Or Are They All Cowboys?

Cattle and horses were a great commodity the Spaniards introduced to their colonies. They had herds running long before any other settlers came to America. So it is little wonder that dealing with cattle herding on the open range had to bring forth some new ways of talking about it. Fauna and flora, unusual landforms, and special new equipment had to be given names. In the southwestern United States, on the meeting and mingling of the three major cultural groups, the newcomers from the East Coast drew heavily on Spanish to communicate while disregarding the much too "exotic" native languages.

So there they were, riding over the mesas (tabletop mountains) on a pinto (painted horse), *lazo* (lasso) in one hand looking out over the chaparral (low bushes), crossing some arroyos (dry creeks)—many a vaquero (buckaroo, cowboy) wanting to find that *mesteña* (herd of mustangs). They always were in need of more broncos (wild horses). And they were never safe from desperados. The *cherife* (sheriff), or later on the *rinches* (rangers), couldn't catch every single *bandido* (bandit) and take him to the *juzg(ad)o* (hoosegow = jail).

Long before that, in 1528, the Spanish king (Charles I) had ordered the colonies to raise more horses and cows to help maintain the Spaniards' position of power. At the same time he refused to allow natives to own livestock. Horses were essential in battle as well as impressive in public display. But it proved inevitable that the landowners needed skilled native horsemen to take care of their teeming herds.

When in the following century the mestizo *rancheros*, a new social class, arose, horses had become quite easily available. Riding equipment had been adjusted to new needs in a different environment and for specific purposes. Horses became a status symbol and horsemanship a sport. There was so much pride in owning a good horse that the well-to-do rancheros adorned the harnesses and saddles with silver. The riders wore richly embroidered suits as their Sunday best. However, people of good taste soon turned up their noses at such *charro* (gaudy, boorish) behavior of the nouveau riche.

The word *charros* has stuck with these skilled horsemen until today. And the competitions of these "cowboys" have turned into a much revered national pastime, the *charrerías*, somewhat akin to the popular rodeos in Canada and the United States.

Related Web links: nacionaldecharros.com— website of the National Charro Association (S); tpwd.state.tx.us/park/jose/vaquero.htm— vaqueros in Texas (E)

Mexicanismos

Español, or to be more precise, *el castellano*, is the official language of Mexico. About three-quarters of the 100 million population speak it on a daily basis. The other 28 percent communicate mostly in the indigenous languages of Nahuatl (the old Aztec language), Maya, Purépecha, Tarahumara, Otomí, Zapotec, Totonac, and many others. All those speak Spanish as well, and many are to a certain degree bilingual.

Mexican Spanish differs quite a bit from the peninsular Spanish of Spain. Most noticeable are the substitution of the "vosotros" ("you guys") forms for "ustedes" and the absence of the peninsular lisp. Mexico, and the rest of the Spanish-speaking Americas, pronounces the *c* and *z* before the vowels *e* and *i* like an *s*. The most obvious difference, however, is in the lexicon. *Mestizaje*, the thorough meshing of the European and indigenous cultures, has dropped "unneeded" peninsular vocabulary while adding a great many words, names, idiomatic phrases, and culturally unique sayings that show up in dictionaries as *mexicanismos*.

On arrival the Spaniards had to come up with ways to represent the new sounds with written letters. The problem started with the tribal name of the *mexica*, pronounced "me-shee-ka" (Aztecs, later Nahuas). The letter *x*, hardly used in *castellano*, came to represent the *sh* sound (as in English "shop"). Some Spaniards even today hear it rather as the *j* (*jota*) and therefore would spell the word as "mejicas." The confusion goes on to the customary English pronunciation of Mexico, with the letter *x* following the pattern heard in mix or tuxedo, while real *mexicanos* go with what is heard as "me-h-ico."

Concepts unique to the Mexican way of life have also made it into the Latin American dictionary and even across the border to the United States. For example, *huaraches*, a type of Mexican sandal, applies to some American footwear as well as to a sole-shaped tortilla dish. *Cuates*, heard all over Latin America, means friends or buddies, as does *escuincles*, an Aztec word for children.

Besides *mexicanismos*, every region has its unique lexical *-ism*. Peanuts are *cacahuates* in Mexico, but *mani* in South America. *Paltas* in Peru become *aguacates* in Mexico, where a kite is a *papalote* while in Spain it is called a *cometa*. To understand all this, most Mexicans would use *entender* rather than *comprender*, and pick up the phone with a "¿diga?" rather than "¿bueno?" These differences apply further to whole idiomatic phrases, from swearwords to the proper use of language according to traditional etiquette. Asking a child for her name, a most likely answer would be, "*María del Carmen, a sus ordenes* (Maria del Carmen, at your service)."

A word of warning: some words that are harmless elsewhere might mean something else in Mexico or vice versa. In everyday language, *huevos* (eggs) mostly refers to testicles and it is wiser to use the word *blanquillos* (white ones) if you want to talk about eggs. Similarly, the verb *coger* in

LANGUAGE

Spain stands, innocently, for "to catch, to grab," whereas in Mexico it is also used for sexual intercourse.

Talking about *mexicanismos* would be utterly incomplete without mentioning some of the more colorful swearwords. Surprise, anger, frustration could elicit a mild *¡caramba!* (darn) or a weightier *¡chin!*, which innocently substitutes for all forms of the most Mexican verb of all: *chingar* (to screw). The family members of this verb are many: *chingón, chingadera, chingada, chinganazo*. If these are con-nected with *la madre* (mother), it gets worse because *la puta* (she-dog) lurks closely, and who wants to be her *hijo* (son)?

Further, any old stinking he-goat provides the overpowering insult of *cabrón*, with a very strong sexual association, just like *pendejo* (pubic hair). As deeply as all those expressions might insult in certain moments, they can easily become synonyms for *buddy*, etc. So, *¡no te preocupes, buey!* (Don't worry, dude! Actually: ox = castrated bull).

Proverbs, Compliments, and Double Meanings

Proverbios o dichos (proverbs or sayings) are very much alive in Mexico. Just as everywhere else, they concisely affirm universally gained wisdom. They can be tongue-in-cheek funny as well as resigned to the demands of daily life. Through language they are closely tied to specific social groups and culture, but they mostly transcend nationalities. They apply to every human endeavor anywhere, they have been around for generations, and usually do not reflect current conditions.

"*A cada cerdo le llega su San Martín* (To each pig comes its St. Martin)" is about the day of reckoning. Saint Martin's day (November 11) coincides with the days of *las matanzas*, the slaughtering of farm animals for winter provisions.

"Time is money" as a saying does not exist in the traditional Mexican lifestyle. Frequently—and stereotypically—accused of *mañana*-like attitudes, dealing with time is better expressed by "*Más vale tarde que nunca* (Better late than never)," or "*Más vale el paso que dure que el trote que canse* (A steady pace is better than a tiring trot)," and, more universal, "*Poco a poco se va lejos* (Little by little one gets far)."

A gentlemen looking for a lady could always listen to the following controversial advice: "*Gallina vieja hace buen caldo* (Old chicken makes good soup)," or "*Gallo, caballo y mujer, por la raza has de escoger* (Rooster, horse, or woman: you have to choose by class)." And if the choice gets overwhelming, proverbial help is on the way: "*Mas vale un pajaro en mano que cien volando* (One bird in the hand is worth a hundred flying)."

A short sampling of other Mexican sayings quickly confirms the poignant insights into universal knowledge:

- "*Más rápido se coge al mentiroso que al cojo* (The liar is caught quicker than the lame man)."
- "*A quien Dios no le dio hijos, el diablo le dio sobrinos* (To whom God has not given children, the devil gave nieces and nephews)."
- "*Más sabe el diablo por viejo que por diablo* (The devil knows more for being old than for being a devil)."
- "*En boca cerrada no entran moscas* (In a closed mouth enter no flies)."
- "*No hay peor sordo que el que no quiere oír* (There are none so deaf as those who will not hear)."
- "*Quien siembra vientos recoge tempestades* (He who sows wind will harvest storms)."
- "*Marzo ventoso y abril lluvioso hacen a mayo florido y hermoso* (A windy March and rainy April make a beautiful flowering May)."

The majority of these sayings have direct equivalents in English and other languages—not as literal translations, of course, but as an expression of the same universal idea.

Albures (risks, chances) that play on words and phrases are *muy mexicano*. They are sometimes formulaic but often spontaneous and can be friendly, risqué, and insulting. By changing intonation they create a string of metaphors based on double meaning. The purpose is to attack the other **103**

LANGUAGE

person with strong innuendo by using a wide reservoir of synonyms of sexual vocabulary (e.g., *chile, chorizo*) and thus elicit a response.

Albures usually fly back and forth rapidly until one partner runs out of ideas or rolls over laughing. *Albures* that cross the fine line of acceptable limits, not necessarily of crudeness but rather the implied rules of the "art," can sometimes backfire into *autoalbures*.

Most of the time *albures* are very direct and always between males. A question as innocent as "What's your name?" could trigger "*Benito Camelo (Ven y tocamelo* [Come and touch it]")," which is, of course, an open challenge to instantly engage in a battle of *albures*, a contest for which cultural outsiders, or even the most dedicated language learners, need not apply.

Piropos (flirtatious remarks, flatteries, pickup lines) are on the gentler and more presentable side. Again a manly domain, *piropos* can be flowery, creative, and sometimes even secretly appreciated. It is what is whispered into the woman's ear at a dance, said in a first conversation, or yelled at the lady passing by:

- [whistle] "*¡Ay, tantas curvas, y yo sin frenos!* (Wow, so many curves and I with no brakes)"
- [whistle] "*¿De qué juguetería te escapaste, muñexa?* (Which toy store did you escape from, doll?)"
- "*¿Dónde venden los números para ganarse este premio?* (Where do they sell the tickets for that prize?)"

- "*¿Qué hora es? Es que necesito decirle a mi analista el momento exacto en que me volví loco.* (What time is it? I need to tell my counselor the exact moment when I went crazy.)"
- "*Aúnque no te llames Alicia ¿vendrás del país de maravillas?* (Even though your name may not be Alice, are you from Wonderland?)"
- "*¡Cómo avanza la tecnología... hasta las flores caminan!* (How technology advances . . . even flowers are walking!)"
- "*¡Me gustaría bañarme en el cielo de tus ojos!* (I would like to bathe in the sky of your eyes!)"

Piropos can obviously turn slippery and *albures* definitely are. A woman's reaction has traditionally been to avoid eye contact or, rarely, to make a sharp remark, "*Respeten a las mujeres* (Respect women)," and then walk on, stone faced. But the question of awareness of sexual harassment has been raised. Intellectual young women at the major universities have already caught on to *la nueva onda* (the new way of thinking) and don't want to play these games any more. Traditional gender roles, however, are still in place in most rural areas, as they are also, and surprisingly, in the cosmopolitan upper class.

Related Web links: oneproverb.net/bwfolder/
mexicanbw.html—Mexican proverbs translated
into English (E); **inside-mexico.com/proverbs**
.htm—proverbs, riddles (E)

Language Learning: Courses and Schools Abroad

As the debate on the increasing presence of the Spanish language in the United States continues, many students, young professionals, businesspeople, and retired folks take up the challenge to learn Spanish. Community colleges and universities see an increasing number of serious and recreational learners, as well as graduates who hold a degree in Spanish language in combination with another major field of studies. More and more university programs offer a stay abroad, and the "converts" come back and happily engage in bilingual enterprises at home.

The necessity of going away and living in the culture where the language of choice is spoken has become quite clear. For Spanish learners it has created a big industry south of the border as well as in the more distant peninsular Spain. All those schools, appealing to diverse clienteles, promise, across the board, to make their students fluent if they agree to their conditions.

Fluency however, can mean many things on many different levels. The American Council on the Teaching of Foreign Languages (ACTFL) has been working on detailed guidelines to determine a more precise assessment of this elusive label. For example, the Oral Proficiency Interview (OPI) tries to establish a person's abilities in oral communication on a scale from 1 to 10—from novice to superior level. This is not grading an achievement in a particular learning situation, but rather a student's functioning in the target language. This scale covers the wide distance between an absolute beginner and an edu-

cated native speaker of the tested language in plateau increments a certified ACTFL tester is trained to distinguish.

1. Novice Low
2. Novice Mid
3. Novice High
4. Intermediate Low
5. Intermediate Mid
6. Intermediate High
7. Advanced Low
8. Advanced Mid
9. Advanced High
10. Superior

The details of these guidelines show how intricate an assessment can be. Here is an excerpt of the description of Level 5 (intermediate–mid) speakers who have attempted to conquer a language other than their native tongue, in any kind of learning situation.

Intermediate-Mid: Speakers are able to express personal meaning by creating with the language, in part by combining and recombining known elements and conversational input to make utterances of sentence length and some strings of sentences. Their speech may contain pauses, reformulations, and self-corrections as they search for adequate vocabulary and appropriate language forms to express themselves. Because of inaccuracies in their vocabulary and/or pronunciation and/or grammar and/or syntax, misunderstandings can occur, but Intermediate-Mid speakers are generally understood by sympathetic interlocutors accustomed to dealing with non-natives. (ACTFL guidelines)

LANGUAGE

This is where, by the way, and optimistically, a motivated language learner may end up after four years of instructional sequence in secondary education.

The chances of moving up on the ACTFL scale increases dramatically by immersion in the environment where the target language is spoken. It brings in one of the most important but often neglected components of language proficiency: the underlying culture. Listening, speaking, reading, and writing all depend on it and are nothing without it.

A good language school in any Spanish-speaking country will capitalize on this fact. It will first of all assess the students' entry level, put them up with families who want to interact with them, and include them in their activities. It will not waste time in lengthy and busy book work but rather engage the students in meaningful and locally relevant issues presenting language structure through "embedded" culture—that is, no subjunctive without relating it to the daily life of the student. It will also provide ample time, ideally one-on-one situations with locals, granting the students an opportunity to see their new environment through the eyes of a native while constantly and actively pushing the limits of their communicative skills.

The mirrored advice for the prospective language learner is quite obvious: immerse yourself in the language and culture, embrace the experience, constantly reach out, and fight your comfort zone. Party with the locals, and stay away from the students you came with!

Related Web links: studyspanish.com/schools— lists of language schools in Spanish-speaking countries (E); **sipuebla.com**—Spanish Institute of Puebla, with online placement test and many other links (E)

Etiquette and Social Interaction

"¡*Con permiso!*" is the phrase most heard in crowded public places, the equivalent of "excuse me" in the United States when space is tight "¡*Despues de usted!* (After you)" is common when a doorway is crowded, and "¡*Perdóneme!*" when toes are stepped on. All cultures share these particular basic formalities, as they do other kindnesses and behavior rules that make human interaction easier and more pleasant. Each culture has developed its own unique modalities and fine registers of dos and don'ts that are not easily available to the newcomer or casual tourist.

Various components contribute to how Mexicans behave. For one there is the Spanish influence, then the multicultural crucible of ethnic diversity, and third the dominant religion: three demands for high standards of respect and honor, dignity, and morals.

The Spanish conquistadors and nobility left an indelible imprint by emphasizing *el pundonor* (the stance of honor, saving face). This attitude has two sides to it: protecting the clan's honor with a total devotion to family interests as well as pursuing any quest that may arise from that very obligation. These attitudes survive somewhat in macho behavior as well as the respect that men pay to women or how a subordinate deals with the boss. Abuse can then be seen as an attempt to reinstate lost honor and respect. Benito Juárez ingeniously summarized these attitudes that are necessary for harmonious coexistence in his famous quote: "Respect for the other person's rights means peace." As an indigenous Mexican he also very much stood for dignity. It is easy to perceive this self-contained nobility in interaction with Mexico's native population. Nothing can damage this poise, neither abject poverty nor social injustice.

Catholicism has added Christian ethics, the Ten Commandments, and a thick layer of traditions, customs, social patterns, and humility. "*Si Dios quiere* (God willing)" or "*Dios primero* (God first)" are humbly attached to any spoken future plans. Saying that is an integral part of the etiquette, making the speaker appear modest at the same time as relieving him of responsibility.

Social interaction is further characterized by personal space and physical contact. An informal study compared people from different nationalities getting together in a coffeehouse for a pleasant conversation; within five minutes the Italians touched and nudged each other forty-seven times, the Spaniards thirty-one times, the French twenty-three times, the Germans nine times, and the British once — accidentally. The Mexicans come between the Spaniards and French. Also, while Americans get uncomfortable when a stranger or casual acquaintance intrudes on their personal space (± 20 inches, or 50 cm), Latin Americans can generally easily handle half of that without retreating or feeling that their intimate space has been invaded.

Greeting each other depends very much on this question of distance. A handshake followed by *un abrazo* (a friendly hug with shoulder patting), is very common between acquaintances, friends, and even business partners. Women and girls kiss each other once on the cheek; men do the same if they know the lady.

Children participate in the social scene of the family very actively and learn very quickly how to behave as an adult. Respect, which takes an important place in their education at home, is expressed through posture (as body language), *los modales* (manners) at the table, and their interaction with family members, friends, adults, the opposite sex, their peers and employees, with strangers, at celebrations, in school, in public, in dressing, in conversation, and how to address people.

Therefore, a well-educated Mexican can appear very suave. He will be courtly polite to ladies (open the car door, adjust her chair, find the best seat, pay the bill), be very caring to his mother and other relatives, and be kind with children. If this doesn't quite fit the picture of a more general perception, it is due solely to inequities in the socioeconomic structure.

USEFUL PHRASES FOR POLITE INTERACTION:

¡Buenos días!	Good morning! (until noon)
¡Buenas tardes!	Good day/evening! (after twelve noon)
¡Buenas noches!	Good night!
¡Hola!	Hi!
¡Hasta luego!	See you later!
¡Hasta mañana!	See you tomorrow!
¡Adios!	Good bye!

Por favor	Please
¡Gracias!	Thanks!
¡De nada! ¡No hay de que!	Don't mention it!
¡Oiga señor/señora/ señorita!	Excuse me, Sir/ Madam/Miss!
¡Mucho gusto conocerle!	Pleasure to meet you!
¡El gusto es mío!	The pleasure is mine!
¡Con permiso!	With your permission!
¡Perdóneme!	Pardon me! Excuse me!
¡Pase Usted!	Go ahead!
¡Mande?	Beg your pardon,
¡No entiendo!	I don't understand!
¡Lo siento!	Bless you!/ Gesundheit! (after someone sneezes)
¿Cómo está Usted?/ ¿Cómo le va?	How are you?
Bien, gracias.	Fine, thanks.
¡Muy amable!	Very nice (of you)!
¡Buena suerte!/ ¡Qué le vaya bien!	Good luck!
¡Qué se divierta!	Have fun!

Related Web links: workabroad.monster.com/ articles/mexiquette—general guidelines on social behavior (E); executiveplanet.com/ business-etiquette/Mexico.html—general guidelines on business etiquette (E)

Reading

There are an estimated three million Internet users in Mexico today. *Los cibercafés* abound and have taken over many of the obsolete fax outlets. While 3 percent of the population is now connected electronically, most people still get their information through radio, TV, and print.

Reading for pleasure has traditionally been suppressed by the need for total devotion to earning a living, and even leading metropolitan newspapers cannot sell more than 100,000 to 200,000 copies in the Mexico City area of twenty million people. This prompted the SEP to promote the reading of the great classics of world literature. They found an unlikely partner in the transportation authorities and police department of Mexico City. Collaborating with advertising companies, they printed 1.5 million special editions of short masterworks of world literature — prose, poems, and plays — and distributed them in the subway stations of Mexico City. Over the next two years, six million more copies will be made available. It is a first-come, first-served, "take one and read while you are riding the Metro" approach, generously tied to an honor system of returning the book when finished before picking up the next one. The hope was to improve the social attitudes of citizens while reducing the crime rate. A big player in this campaign was Rudolph Giuliani, former mayor of New York, whose firm was invited to help Mexico's capital become a safer place. Last heard, the return rate was approximately 60 percent.

The literacy rate in Mexico is 90 percent, but like anywhere else, actual functional literacy is much lower. Publishers take account of this and provide their customers with a wide selection of not-so-challenging reading materials, such as *fotonovelas* (little booklets with photographed picture stories and speech bubbles); *periódicos* (newspapers) with extensive *gacetillas* (gossip, social events); *revistas* (magazines) like *¡Alarma!*, which appeals to the lowest instincts with uncensored reality spreads showing horrendous photos of mangled victims of accidents and crimes. Appealing to a totally different reader, *México desconocido* (*Unknown Mexico*), which explores areas off the beaten path, their traditions and folklore. As for *las noticias* (the news), *América-Economía* deals in depth with special issues relevant to Latin America.

At the numerous *quioscos* (newsstands) all over the country, many magazines from abroad are sold in Spanish translation: *Geografía nacional, Cosmopolitan, People en español, Historia natural,* and *Newsweek en español,* and more. The national and international scene of royalty, film, sports, and TV stars, is covered by *Cristina,* Mexico's very own Oprah.

Although national politics appears to be covered sufficiently by the press, Mexicans have been lulled into political apathy over the last three generations under the PRI, a party that barely listened to the people. Under their rule, reporting anything different from the party-sanctioned version of news was not tolerated. Then, reporters were given their scripts and *embutes,* envelopes stuffed with bribe money to be shared with the editors. Since the late

1990s, during the decline of the PRI-dominated government, this practice has become impractical, and papers like the leftist *La Jornada*, now free from harrassment, have become more responsible and moderate. The need for vicious attacks born from frustration has diminished as transparency in the political process increases.

THE TOP TEN MEXICAN NEWSPAPERS BASED ON NATIONWIDE SALES

1. *El universal*
2. *El sol de México*
3. *Reforma*
4. *El sol de Tijuana*
5. *El excelsior*
6. *El heraldo de México*
7. *La crónica de hoy*
8. *La voz de la frontera*
9. *Novedades*
10. *Diario de México*

THE TOP TEN MEXICAN MAGAZINES BASED ON NATIONWIDE SALES

1. *AméricaEconomía*
2. *Clara*
3. *Mujer ejecutiva*
4. *Homopolitan*
5. *Revista equis*
6. *Olé México gay*
7. *Deportes 15/30*
8. *México desconocido*
9. *Planeta X*
10. *The Travel Guide*

Related Web links: el-universal.com.mx, elsoldemexico.com.mx, reforma.com—newspaper websites (S); americaeconomica.com, semexico.com—magazine websites (S)

Film and TV

The end of the millennium saw the demise of the once prosperous Mexican film industry. After a short burst of creativity in the 1970s, government-instituted film-making and young hopefuls were stifled by the cumbersome red tape of bureaucracy.

One of the first directors to break away from government sponsorship was Alejandro Gonzáles with a movie named *Amores perros* (2000). Although very much located in "el DF" (Distrito Federal, Mexico City), he wanted to create a universal metaphor that could be understood throughout the Hispanic world and beyond. *Tough Love* (an interpretive translation of the title) has become a milestone in filmmaking as it does not celebrate violence so much as depict it as an integral part of living in the monstrous metropolis of Mexico City.

More recently, Alfonso Cuarón took an even more controversial look at Mexican society with *Y tu mamá también* in 2001. He did this so convincingly that he was offered the job of directing one of the Harry Potter sequels, *Harry Potter and the Prisoner of Azkaban*, which he did very successfully. In 2002 Carlos Carrera made *Los crímenes del padre Amaro*, released in the United States as *The Crimes of Padre Amaro*. Along came the multitalented musician, designer, and filmmaker Sergio Arau, son of Alfonso Arau, himself a prominent Mexican film director. Sergio, a graduate of the prestigious National School of Film (CUEC) in Mexico City, with one of his first feature film topics ventured across the border to California for *Un día sin Mexicanos* (*A Day Without Mexicans*), released in 2004.

All these recent successful efforts in producing movies that can survive in the domestic, NAFTA, and international markets without government support has boosted the interest of Mexican investors and has helped promote further attempts. Especially when there are actors like Salma Hayek and Jennifer Lopez and heartthrobs like Gael Garcia Bernal, who was not only featured in three of the movies already mentioned but also stars in *Los diarios de motocicleta* (*The Motorcycle Diaries*), a Brazilian production of 2004, as the young Che Guevara.

Mexico has always been one of the most important and prolific sources of film in Latin America. Luis Buñuel set high standards with avant-garde movies that often focused on social issues in Mexico, such as *Los olvidados* (*The Forgotten*). In the second half of the last century there was a shift to lighter entertainment, and the period now referred to nostalgically as *la época de oro* (the golden age) still resonates in our times. This period brought an abundance of movies exulting the *charro*, the romance of life on the ranch, love, and the painful limits of social barriers — although they can now appear slightly corny. Nevertheless, many actors of that time have made it into the popular hall of fame, among them María Félix, Pedro Armendáriz, the brothers Soler, and the two immortal tenors of that time, Pedro Infante and Jorge Negrete, who often played the romantic horsemen who could sing their way into the heart of *las señoritas*, complete their quests, and then ride off into the sunset. And one should not forget the legendary Mario Moreno Cantínflas, who has given moviegoers a welcome escape from their harsh reality for the last thirty years.

The past and future of Mexican film-making are closely tied to Los Estudios Churrubusco Azteca, formerly a government-subsidized complex of film studios in Mexico City. Today it is privatized and on a par with its two major competitors in the Latin world, Metrovisión in Argentina and Globo in Brazil. It is a facility that offers ample space and technology to any aspiring filmmaker with enough financial backing. It is also home to the prolific Mexican *telenovela* productions that are very popular all over the Americas, as well as for the endless production of TV commercials.

The big TV networks of Mexico have recently been reaching across the northern border. Univision (owned by Televisa), Telemundo (owned by NBC), and TVAzteca are already well established in the United States, and some are also reaching out to collaborate with Brazilian and Argentinean networks. Their programming has acquired a more Pan-American character by dropping linguistic regionalism and adjusting the types of offerings to an international standard. The news anchor Jorge Ramos personifies that approach, as had Jacobo Zabludovsky before him. And Mario Kreuzberger (aka Don Francisco), the Chilean host of an eclectic Saturday night quiz show, *El sábado gigante*, has proven over and over again that programs can preserve their own unique Latino character without being absorbed into the American way. Don Francisco has actually become so popular with his viewers that he was chosen for the formal Spanish interviews of the U.S. presidential candidates in 2004.

Related Web links: univision.net (E, S), telemundo.com (S), tvazteca.com (S)—TV channel websites; mexicochannel.net—media links (E)

Communication

The people of Atzacoalotepec still wake up every morning to the sounds of *la máquina*, a loudspeaker mounted on a long pole close to the municipal offices at the town square. The announcements at dawn usually start with best wishes to the day's birthday celebrants followed by scratchy and static renditions of "Las mañanitas," the birthday song. Then come other general announcements concerning the community, with the background explosions of *los cohetes*, sometimes dynamite-laced firecrackers, to wake up the birthday child.

This scenario is, without doubt, disappearing all over rural Mexico due to quantum leaps in ever-improving technology in telecommunications. Some areas went straight from mid-1900s technology to *la red*, the Internet. Solar panels are complementing gas generators as energy sources in remote areas, and satellite dishes bring in hundreds of TV channels from all over the world.

The Zapatista movement in Chiapas has clearly shown how e-technology can win worldwide support and, therefore, drastically increase leverage in the domestic arena. The Internet has become an essential tool for democratization, worldwide.

The privatizing of the national telephone services in 1990 quickly improved national and international services. Telmex has become the main player, and its CEO, Carlos Slim, one of the richest billionaires in Mexico. América Móvil, 65 percent owned by one family, has branched out to encompass forty-four million subscribers from the Río Grande to Tierra del Fuego.

Lately both Telmex and América Movil have faced challenges from their government's antitrust laws, but have been very successful in defending their huge share of the telecommunications market and securing future business.

In general, the telephone service still needs major improvement for the general population in Mexico. For the 103 million citizens there are now about sixteen million main lines available, although cellular phone use, according to some statistics, has exploded from two million in 1997 to twenty-six million in 2003. While access to fax machines has provided good opportunities for small business (*fax público*) in rural areas during the late 1990s it is now the *cibercafé* that has taken over. By the year 2000, around two hundred Internet service providers served four million Internet users, a number that continues to grow in leaps and bounds. Meanwhile, radio and television is growing much more slowly. About 1,500 radio stations broadcast to thirty-one million radios, 240 television stations to twenty-six million TVs.

In keeping pace with global communication technology, Mexico is constantly developing new and better access at home and internationally: earth stations for satellite systems, microwave radio relay networks, and the use of fiberoptic cable hooking up with the Americas as well as Europe and Africa.

Related Web links: telmex.com.mx, america movil.com.mx—telephone company websites (S)

The National Symbol

The coat of arms waves with the wind on *la bandera* (the flag). Framed by the colors green, red, and white, it tells the story of the brave Aztecs over and over again—how they fulfilled their destiny in the slow migration from the north to the shores of Lake Texcoco, where their shaman Tenoch saw his dream materialize: the island with an eagle holding a snake in its beak and talons, perched on a cactus. On that site they built their city, which within two hundred years became the base of the powerful Aztec empire.

Another, less well-known legend tells an older story that might well have been the background of Tenoch's dream. According to that version, the Aztecs had already settled down on Chapultepec Hill. Amongst them was a sorceress who claimed to be the sister of Huitzilopochtli, the mighty god of the Aztecs, who had shamelessly abandoned her.

Years later she had a son whom she named Cópil. When he had grown to be a warrior he wanted to avenge his mother's lifelong grievance by openly insulting Huitzilopochtli and defacing his temple. The indignant god ordered one of the high priests to silence Cópil and toss his heart into the reeds by the lake.

Soon, out of Cópil's heart grew a nopal, a prickly pear cactus, on which an eagle landed to devour the snake—all of which Tenoch recognized as the setting of his dream. And thus Tenochtitlán, "the place of Tenoch," became the new home of the Aztecs.

This symbol had been painted on codices in pictographic accounts of Aztec history long before the conquest in 1521. Nowadays this *escudo* (coat of arms) is found everywhere as the official national emblem on coins, government letterheads and buildings, postage stamps, army trucks, and lottery tickets. It has gained in importance as Mexico's turbulent history progressed. In the struggle for independence and during revolutions it has spurred the indigenous spirit and asserted the native component in the mestizo soul.

On September 16, 1968, the flag with its current design was officially hoisted, although since 1921 all the former versions had displayed the same components. Green still stands for *la independencia* (independence), white for *la pureza* (purity of religion), and red for *la sangre* (the union of Spanish, Indians, and those of mixed blood).

Related Web link: surfnetkids.com/games/ mexico-utjs.htm—Mexican flag jigsaw puzzle (E)

Three Cultures at La Plaza de Las Tres Culturas

To understand the turmoil that dwells in the mestizo soul can, according to Mexico's premier writer, Nobel laureate, and philosopher, Octavio Paz, probably best be understood by visiting La Plaza de Las Tres Culturas in Tlatelolco, Mexico City. It was there that Cortés defeated Cuauhtémoc, the last Aztec emperor, in 1521. In the twentieth century it became what it is now—the physical/architectural manifestation of the fusion of two nations into a new third nation. A plaque in the square commemorates that historical battle: "There was no victory or defeat. It was the painful birth of the mestizo nation that is Mexico today."

Nowadays, the square is a somber and quiet place where the three architectural components emphasize the diversity of the social makeup of present-day Mexico.

First, there are the ruins of an Aztec temple that once formed part of a huge ceremonial center of Tenochtitlán's sister city of Tlatelolco and the most important trade center at the time of the arrival of the Spaniards.

Then, soon after the conquest, the Spaniards built right on top of the original building the colonial Franciscan monastery, including a somber church dedicated to Santiago, their patron saint. The building materials came, as was usual in those days, directly from the Aztec site that had been dismantled by the Spanish soldiers. This site became a most important religious center, the headquarters of the

Plaza de Las Tres Culturas, D.F.

"conversion campaign," where many indigenous people were baptized and subsequently indoctrinated with Catholicism. One of those Indians was Juan Diego from Tepeyac who, in 1531, received the apparitions of Nuestra Señora de Guadalupe (Our Lady of Guadalupe), the most revered patron saint of Mexico.

The third and modern part of the whole picture is made up from the straight lines of apartment buildings and the offices of the secretariat of foreign affairs.

Here in 1968, in La Plaza de Las Tres Culturas, the conflict among the three cultures—or better, the three political and economic groups—boiled over and ended in a bloody massacre. On the eve of the Olympic Games government troops opened fire on protesters while the whole world watched. Around three hundred protesters were killed, and the government swept all evidence under the carpet. Decades later, details of that sad night are still kept in top-secret archives and continue to haunt the government. It is in many ways Mexico's own Tiananmen Square.

If the visitor today, standing in that square, can absorb and integrate all those elements in his mind, then he might probably for a moment understand the complexity of the Mexican soul.

Related Web link: geocities.com/CapitolHill/
Lobby/3231/RSM/tlatelolco-eng.html—account
of the 1968 massacre (E)

National Heroes: Children, Politicians, Priests, and a Nun

Public monuments, banknotes, coins, street names, history books, and holidays offer a pretty good idea of who, throughout history, were a nation's figureheads. Some of those citizens rose to legendary status not only through accomplishments in politics and the military, but also through other remarkable contributions to national, and often universal, cultural traditions.

On the eastern edge of El Parque de Chapultepec, Mexico City's biggest park, right below the castle stands the monument to *los niños héroes* (the heroic boys). It pays homage to six cadets of the Colegio Militar (military academy) who gave their life for their country during the Mexican-American War of 1846–1848. The death of those thirteen- to nineteen-year-olds in 1847 has become the purest expression of patriotism in Mexican history. The American troops were about to take Chapultepec Hill when these six cadets who had been left behind saw no way out. Wrapped in the Mexican flag, they threw themselves off the roof and down the steep hill. They died obeying to the fullest the law of the academy: death before surrender.

And if to be a hero means giving your life for the cause, Mexico has a long list of formidable heroes who put the common good above their own. In the night of September 15, 1810, the parish priest of a village in the present state of Guanajuato, Father Miguel Hidalgo, shouted out *¡independencia!* and *¡muerte a los gachupines!* (death to the Spaniards), which of course went with it, to his parishioners. For initiating the independence movement he not only has become a national icon but also joins rank with other *libertadores* (liberators) — George Washington, Simon Bolívar, San Martín, O'Higgins, and others. Many more men could be lined up next to Hidalgo: Guerrero, Morelos, Zapata, Obregón, Carranza, Juárez . . . but where are the women?

In 1667, at the age of 16, Juana, a young lady obsessed with reading and writing, entered a convent, the only place a woman with intellectual ambitions could go. There she read and wrote until her superiors, shocked by her writings and ideas, took her quills away. She died in 1695, but in her short career she had managed to compose some beautiful poetry that Mexicans throughout the ages have memorized: "*Hombres necios que acusais... ,*" and, as Sor Juana Inés de la Cruz, she has become an early model for women's liberation in the New World.

Related Web links: mexconnect.com/mex_/ history/mexicopeople.html—time line of famous Mexicans, with biographies (E); dartmouth.edu/ ~sorjuana—images and biography of Sor Juana Inés de la Cruz (E)

Benito Juárez

Aeropuerto Internacional Benito Juárez in Mexico City is Mexico's major gateway to the world. Naming it after Don Benito Juárez (1806–1872) indicates the reverence his *compatriotas* feel for this ninteenth-century politician. His accomplishments in national reforms — stripping the church of its power and stopping the French intervention by putting the Hapsburg prince Maximilian, Napoleon's "puppet emperor," in front of a firing squad — exemplifies a type of patriotism that is still cherished by the whole nation.

He means different things to each stratum of society. For the indigenous Mexicans, Benito Juárez has clearly shown by example how to overcome poverty and ignorance. To the middle class he taught that big power can be broken and wealth can be redistributed. For the big land owners he left a very clear message that their workers must be respected and included if they wanted to keep their holdings.

Juárez was born a Zapotec Indian in the village of San Pablo Guelateo in the state of Oaxaca on March 21, 1806. He learned Spanish at the age of thirteen when he came to live with the Maza family in the town of Oaxaca. There he attended school and was about to train for the priesthood in a Franciscan seminary. His real interest, however, was the law, politics, and philosophy. By 1834 he had become so involved with the thoughts of the rationalist philosophers of the enlightenment that he eventually rejected Catholicism.

He served in local government, twice as the governor of Oaxaca, and was eventually swept into the federal government. His *ley de Juárez* (1857) abolished the immunity of the Church and triggered the *guerra de la reforma* (War of Reform), 1858 to 1861. In that struggle the all-powerful church lost its stronghold on the country and all its worldly possessions were expropriated.

Juárez was president of the republic, on and off, from 1858 to 1872, with long periods of interruption due to internal and external interventions. As a statesman Juárez is often compared to Abraham Lincoln or Winston Churchill. He is remembered on banknotes (presently the 20-peso bill) and many monuments around Mexico, the most elaborate being the *hemiciclo de Juárez* (the Juárez semicircle) in the Alameda Central park in Mexico City. But he has touched and enriched all humankind with his famous quote: "*El respecto al derecho ajeno es la paz* (Respect for others' rights means peace)."

Related Web link: mcf-festival.com/benito
_juarez.htm—biography and national holiday
(E, S)

118

La Virgen de Guadalupe: Our Lady of Guadalupe

Her picture is everywhere, dangling from rearview mirrors, on necklaces, on street vendors' carts, tattooed on a bulging biceps, and even on bordello walls. Her name is whispered in desperation, shouted in anger and fear, and recited over and over in endless rosaries. She is the ultimate consolation and shelter for the destitute and miserable and much respected by the rich and powerful. She is Mexico's very own madonna—as her mestizo appearance and location of apparitions sufficiently indicate. She, La Virgen de Guadalupe, will protect all her "children."

In 1531 she appeared repeatedly to a newly converted young Aztec peasant, baptized and renamed Juan Diego, on the hill of Tepeyac, north of Mexico City. Juan Diego's former name, Cuauhtlatoahtzin (the eagle who speaks), implies probably more than the legend suggests: he may have been a nobleman from the ranks of the Aztec Eagle Warriors with social ties and credibility necessary to gain access to Juan de Zumárraga, then archbishop of Mexico City.

From him the Virgin demanded that a church be built in her honor. It took a miracle, however, to finally convince Archbishop Zumárraga. It was not until Juan Diego brought roses wrapped in his *tilma* (poncho) in the cold of winter that the archbishop became a willing listener. And then, when the *tilma* showed the image of La Virgen, the legend took hold.

Did all this really happen, or is the story pure invention? For one, history proves that in the miracle of Tepeyac the Catholic missionaries found their most powerful vehicle for the conversion of the Mexican people. That it happened where the Aztecs had long venerated Tonantzín (mother of gods) might be a coincidence or a mere spiritual parallel to physically putting a church on top of a pyramid.

To witness the adoration that Mexico grants La Virgen, one has to go to La Villa, the present location of the shrine of Guadalupe, north of Mexico City, where every day pilgrims arrive from all over the country to pray to La Virgen and catch a glimpse of the image on the well-preserved *tilma*, framed in gold, in the new cathedral.

But every December 12 religious fervor comes to a boil. It's the *santo* (name day) of La Virgen de Guadalupe. On foot, in buses and cars, and on bicycles, pilgrims arrive to pay their respects to the virgin and attend masses, some after enduring extreme hardships, walking for weeks, and approaching the shrine for the last kilometers on their knees. Blood, sweat, and tears in exchange for eternal reward.

Related Web link: interlupe.com.mx—
information from the Center for Guadalupan
Studies (E, S)

The Cross and the Sword: Roman Catholicism in Mexico

Today about 90 percent of the Mexican population claims to be *católico*. This statistic, however, is not based on a count of tithe-paying parishioners but rather on the numbers not officially belonging to any other religion. The main flock still follows the rites and rules imposed centuries ago by the Spanish conquerors and missionaries.

In the beginning the Aztecs must have felt quite bewildered. On the one hand they were told about the all-encompassing love of a merciful and forgiving God, while on the other they were being brutally herded up to do slave labor for their sword-wielding patrons—a contradiction that would forever cast a shadow on any interaction between the Spanish and the Mexicans.

Mexicans quickly learned to go through the necessary liturgical motions without losing their stoic attitudes. It is therefore hard to judge how thick the Catholic veneer actually might be. The long conversion process produced some quite remarkable monuments, from the colonial heartland to the outposts of the kingdom. A few striking examples of this struggle can be found in Cholula, where a church was ostentatiously built on top of the Tepanapa pyramid, or in Tonantzintla, where the European baroque is splendidly redefined in a complex fusion with the indigenous artisans' skills and sense of color.

Because of its overarching power, the Church has met strong opposition and was challenged by the secular authorities. In the nineteenth century, President Benito Juárez separated church and state. Religious orders were prohibited and monasteries had to be abandoned. But if these measures aimed to eliminate the influence of the church, they succeeded only superficially.

Over the years the mestizos had become the most pious followers of what the conquistadors had preached. The traditions connected with the churches built with the sweat and blood of their ancestors became focal points of their communities. As a result, Catholicism is so embedded in Mexican society that it is inseparable from its folkloric traditions. It dominates human life from *el bautismo* through *primera comunión, confirmation, la quinceañera,* and *la boda* (the wedding ceremony), to the last rites and funeral. The priest is always there, representing the Church.

And church is also ultimately where the downtrodden and unprivileged masses will turn to for the comfort and consolation that no worldly authority can, or is willing to, give. And, "*Si Dios quiere, ¿quien sabe?* (God willing, who knows?)": miracles may happen at any time!

Related Web link: catholic-hierarchy.org/ country/mx.html—Catholic hierarchy and diocese in Mexico (E)

Catholic Life

Churches dominate everyday life. Architecturally they tower over most communities and are part of the national *patrimonio*, sights proudly shown to tourists. The bells provide the acoustic rhythm to everyday life. They ring out loud for morning mass, at noon, for the Angelus, and for baptisms, weddings, funerals, and catastrophes. They call to the believers and remind everybody of their moral duties. At the same time they promote awareness of continuity, community, obligation, and moments of meditation. *Los curas* (the priests) still hold a strong position in society and haven't faced the degree of scrutiny experienced by their colleagues in the United States and Europe.

Religion in Latin America is not as social as it is in the United States, with its Sunday school and cookies and punch after mass. Rather, it provides the believer with a rather anonymous approach to address his own spiritual needs in private discourse with the divine hierarchy, foremost his favorite saint.

"*Santo que no es visto no es adorado* (A saint not seen is not venerated)" goes the saying. Few are overlooked, and many are part of everyday life in Mexico. However, there are some favorites: the Virgin Mary rules in many different representations. La Virgen de Guadalupe is the number one patron saint not only of Mexico—she is often collectively called *la madre de las Américas*. Argentina and Uruguay have La Virgen de Lujan, Chile has La Virgen del Carmen, Paraguay has Nuestra Señora de la Asunción, and, according to the Vatican, María de la Concepción Imaculada is the patron saint of Brazil and the United States, whereas Santa Rosa de Lima gets to protect at least some parts of South America.

Saints are advocates, the go-betweens; people don't pray *to* them, but ask them to move their concerns and petitions to the highest authority. In a translated sense, they are the poor man's lobbyists. They can't do wrong. Sometimes they are credited when results are good, but they are always forgiven whatever happens. The saints dominate the calendar. Each day of the year has various assigned saints. St. Francis of Assisi is the principal saint on October 4, St. Andrew on August 29, St. Nicholas on December 6, and so on.

So you were born on January 9? In the old days it was pretty likely that you would be named Julian after the saint of the day, San Julian. This way, your birthday would coincide with *el día de tu santo*. And it is still common today to call your birthday your saint's day, even if it isn't. If your name is Jennifer and you were born on June 13 (the day dedicated to San Antonio de Padua), Antonia would have been the traditional choice for your name. According to the new way, however, Jennifer now will celebrate her cumpleaños on June 13 and, additionally, her name day on January 3, the day dedicated to Santa Genoveva (the name etymologically closest to Jennifer).

Saints are ever present, inside churches as *bultos* (statues) or *retablos* (pictures or dioramic scenes) that show, often in shocking realism, the moments of their martyrdom, and therefore the reason why they are saints. Saints are also displayed on dashboards of public buses to protect driver and passengers, on amulets, in everyday speech, and in desperate requests enhanced by a lit candle. San Antonio, for example, is frequently summoned for help in finding lost items. He almost always succeeds, maybe because he grants the searchers enough time to contemplate while they are lighting the candle in front of the statue.

Related Web links: catholic-forum.com/saints/ indexsnt.htm—index of patron saints (E); **vivasancarlos.com/Calendar.html**—calendar of Mexican fiestas (E)

Cholula with Popocatépetl

Health and Medicine

armacias are the little man's place in case of ailment, sickness, or any other troubling symptoms. There he can find an educated, very experienced pharmacist who knows what to dispense. When in doubt, he has a big book that will tell him what to do or recommend. He cannot prescribe drugs, but he'll find some remedy from the shelves. Many *farmacias* also have a back room where some very basic, if not quite legal, examinations can take place. If the right cure is not found, most patients would probably move on to modern medical care, a doctor's office, a clinic, or a hospital.

Rural patients in the remote mountains would first consult with a *curandero*. These healers can be found everywhere, from the jungle of Chiapas to the jungles that are the metropolitan slums, from a tiny market stall in Comitán to the Merced market in the capital. Their merchandise includes herbs, incense, teas, an air-dried burro fetus, bat eyes, and more. They don't know the word "bronchitis," but they know how to cure it. Their recommended treatment prescribes pictures of saints, certain aromatic candles, oils, and specific prayers. The *curandero* also offers cleansing of body, soul, and house. And if necessary, he also can reverse the curse of sickness wished on you by a disgruntled lover, rival, or vicious neighbor.

Serious illness will eventually bring a patient to a rural clinic or hospital, where the medical personnel—a doctor or a nurse practitioner—will examine the patient in a sanitary environment and choose appropriate further treatment according to which category he or she belongs in the social security system.

The social security program of the Instituto Mexicano de Seguro Social (IMSS) covers about 80 percent of the formal workforce that is duly registered and statistically accounted for. That includes various subcategories: state and government workers, national defense employees, members of the navy, Pemex workers, and many more. But a great number of Mexicans—about 56 percent by IMSS counts—exist below the poverty line and belong to the "open population" eligible to be helped by government funds in various programs, but not at all to the full extent of benefits to which members of the IMSS are entitled.

Most businesses, small and large, can buy into the social security system, as can individuals. For a reasonable fee (about US$300 per annum), one can sign up for lifelong coverage and be taken care of by the public health-care system. This is by no means a third-world affair, but a no-nonsense, often wait-in-line, first-come-first-served consultation with doctors who maintain a private office for private patients on alternate days. As a matter of fact, many Americans come to Mexico to study medicine in Guadalajara, Monterrey, and Mexico City before going back to the United States to be licensed to practice there.

For those who are independently wealthy, private medical practice is available and internationally competitive. As mentioned, many doctors throughout the country split their time between the IMSS and their own private office.

SOCIAL ISSUES

Along the northern border many dentists have set up practice to cater to Americans who don't want, or can't afford, treatment at home. There, for a posted fee, it's all possible. Even physicians are available to examine patients and prescribe medicine that can be picked up around the corner at the *farmacia* at a fraction of the price it would cost north of the border.

For tourists or expatriates not accustomed to the Mexican environment it's probably wise to come prepared, bringing along their own medicine and an insurance policy as a lifeline to their home base. But should it become necessary, Mexico is certainly ready to take care of any medical needs.

Related Web link: countrystudies.us/mexico/ 63.htm—health care and social security in Mexico (E)

Racism

Watching TV in Mexico, *telenovelas* (soap operas) and beyond, one cannot ignore the fact that the people in the street look quite different from the image of Mexico portrayed on TV. Why so many blond actresses with their jet-set suitors? Could it be racism? Most people might instantly come up with a correlation between their own economic status and race. But then, somebody says, most of us are mestizos. At that instant, another woman casually mentions that her ancestry is 75 percent or more Spanish as she sails out into the sun, well protected by her parasol to keep her white skin from darkening too much.

Racism in Mexico has never been brought to the conscious level of the electorate enough to cause government action, legislation, or a supreme court to look into racial abuses. In Mexico it always seems to be an economic issue. As it turns out, the *criollos*, Mexican-born descendants of the Spanish conquerors, are still pretty much in charge. Often in powerful positions, they subscribe to the outside influences from Europe and the United States as part of the Western international consumer society, and this they disseminate directly and indirectly all across the nation. Their culture becomes desirable to many, and by subscribing to it, mestizos become accomplices in discrimination they themselves suffer.

So, the Revolution with its demand for *tierra y libertad* was fought for the good of those of mixed heritage, and schoolbooks exalt the Aztec and Mayan ancestors and their heroic efforts against the conquerors. All this visible pride in the Aztec past is spectacularly displayed in the famous Museo Nacional de Antropología in Mexico City and evidenced by the massive income received from visitors to Chichén Itzá in Yucatán. But none of the admiration for these heroic indigenous groups is given to their living descendants.

Racism actually might be too strong a word. It is rather total disregard for the different socioeconomic levels in a society that still shows the imprint of early colonial times. Back then, the *indios* were not allowed to own horses or land, were forced into conversion to Catholicism, and learned to be tolerant of their white-skinned landlords. In southern Mexico, for many years, the indigenous people were simply *there*. Their rising anger against continuing social and economic disregard hardly registered among the governing *criollos*. This indifference was certainly somewhat shaken by the Zapatista uprising in the early 1990s, but those in charge reacted in the customary way of the conquistador, not realizing that the age of the worldwide informational web had dawned, and social and racial problems can no longer be solved by force.

Related Web link: wais.stanford.edu/Mexico/ mexico_racism2.html—short discussion of racism in Mexico (E)

Being a Woman in Mexico

It's a relentless game between *el macho* and *la hembra* (man and woman). There has been a slow awakening to modern realities for the five hundred years since Cortés chose La Malinche as his running mate in the conquest of Mexico. Later on, women had some strong advocates in Sor Juana Inés de la Cruz, superb as she was in intellectually outsmarting most men of her generation, and, among others, Frida Kahlo, who, against all odds, could never quite be subdued by her famous husband.

Women slightly outnumber men in population statistics. They live longer, but the majority of them still have to fight fiercely for what seems to come easily to men. This is not restricted to particular socioeconomic classes but is rather based on traditional roles, inherited from both the indigenous cultures and the conquerors' relationship with women. These "values" tend to survive and are still prevalent in the remote rural areas, where women are forced to maintain a traditional role. There, it is not unusual that marriages are arranged, that fourteen-year-old girls become legal barter for promising opportunities and connections in rural wealth. At the same time the justice system is trying to get a grip on sexual abuse and outright rape of women and minors, whose cries for justice are systematically stifled across the ranks of the male-dominated police force and justice system.

As grim as it sounds, women have learned to navigate the system in a most efficient yet nonconfrontational way. They have learned to step back while still holding very tightly to the reins that control their men. The power of the mother, wife, or sister should never be underestimated. Women command a totally different and powerful network and usually win in the end.

Just like anywhere else, women in the urban centers tend to be more aware of opportunities. Nowadays many make it through the *bachillerato*, go on to one of the public or private universities, and end up in respectable and secure jobs. The thinly populated middle class usually succeeds in improving the fate of their daughters beyond their own situation by providing the best schooling they can afford, paying for additional afternoon and evening classes geared toward the practical application of what they learned.

The rural population lags behind. They face the decision of accepting the old ways and the poverty connected to it, or trying to move on physically and mentally. The urban centers seem to be most attractive, sure to fulfill all the promises—until reality sinks in, sitting in a dusty lot of Nezahualcóyotl, the uncharted slums of Mexico City. Then it's again the woman who has to be the strong one, holding the family together, nurturing the children, consoling a frustrated husband who can't find work, and protecting the family from a husband who has taken to drinking, found another woman, or simply disappeared.

At the higher end of the socioeconomic scale, women are more motivated to play along with the foibles of their husbands, their escapades, their well-known (but ignored) *casas chicas*, and their transparent macho games, which, if not discussed, give the *madre de la familia* substantial power in holding the family together.

Being a woman in Mexico, living there or just visiting, means being alert. Men are keenly aware of their role as conquistador and macho, be it burden or obligation. They are always driven, sweet talking, funny, daring, rarely insisting, and, more often than not, retreating, with the satisfaction of having given it their best.

Women in Mexico have learned to ignore all this as they move through everyday life. They have become experts in avoiding eye contact by focusing on the most minimal task on hand, readily offering a cold shoulder to the macho inventing the most creative *piropos*—or just whistling at every skirt that passes.

But then again, should the woman's interest be piqued, it just takes her an instant to convey that message with a subtle eye movement, a fleeting smile, or even displaying exaggerated disdain, which often leads to more forceful further attempts.

Doña María, potter in Atzacoaloyan, Guerrero

Being a Family in Mexico

The logistics of maintaining a coherent family life are straining all levels of society. The family, proclaimed as the strongest unit in the social structure, is weakening under the onslaught of mass media, commercials, and the global environment in general, which plant ideas in people's minds that have not played any role traditionally—for example, the simple need to pay the bills, a fact that has become one determining issue all across the Mexican spectrum. In the following, *la familia Pérez*, a typical family, will appear in different scenarios a family might experience in Mexico.

In the rural areas and in the wildly growing slums around the big cities, the Pérez family is simply left out. Where most are still disconnected from the power grid or any other state or federal infrastructure the Pérez might possibly have *la luz* (light, electricity) for the only light bulb in the house, or to power a blaring radio and probably a TV, but in general they don't have to worry about any dues to the Comisión Federal de Electricidad (CFE) for lack of a billing address.

Sewers, running water, and refrigeration represent a step up in society and are now easily found in and around *los municipios* (county capitals). Subscribing to those conveniences demands that the Pérez first establish a legal presence in both the tax register and the social security system (*el seguro social*), and then create some regular cash flow in a job with a steady income. Permanent employment can be found, but jobs available for the population living under the poverty level pay too little. The prime example is employment in the maquiladoras: US$4 a day cannot take care of a family. Consequently, two or three family members have to work for the family to survive.

Putting the Pérez family into the southern states would deny them even these opportunities. They would have to subsist on small farming, carefully tending to *la milpa*, growing other vegetables, and raising goats, sheep, pigs, chickens, and sometimes a cow. For cash, Señor Pérez, the father, will have to find day work as *un jornalero* or *cargador* (porter); in good years, any of the meager surplus of farm products could be sold at the *tianguis*, the Sunday market in the closest town where they also do their shopping for what their *ranchito* (small farm) cannot provide (sugar, salt, detergent, utensils, tools, clothes, etc.), always beating the prices for what's available at the *tienditas* (little stores) and supermercado. Eventually the family might decide to migrate to the industrial areas or agricultural regions in the northern part of Mexico.

Once there, every aspect of daily life involves the entire Pérez family at either of the above-mentioned levels. *La señora* works as a maid, the father finds odd jobs—on and off—and the children sell *chicle* in the streets and have dropped out of school. The Pérez have a hard time thinking beyond just barely making it. Their aspirations evaporate under the strain of securing the basics, food and shelter; the umbrella known as *la familia* still provides their only palpable economic and social security. But even that network often crumbles when a father abandons the family or becomes an alcoholic. Then, instead of social services, the *compadrazgo* (godfather) system will shelter and take care of the *ahijados* (godchildren).

One notch up, economically, this Pérez family lives in urban areas, father is a professional and holds a decent job in or owns an established business, perhaps a successful *ferretería* (hardware store), or works for the government. They own a car, shop at the supermarket, and their children's education is such a priority that they send them to one of the many private schools. They also have a stake in the financial structure with access to all the services the bank can provide, a privilege a solvent status can grant. Yet the powerful banks are not quite ready to instantly give loans to those trying to start a small business.

On top of the socioeconomic pyramid the last Pérez family leads an extravagant life in a huge compound in San Ángel or Las Lomas de Chapultepec, with a guarded door and surrounded by high walls. An army of servants—gardeners, chauffeurs, nannies—makes the household run smoothly, under the ever-watchful eyes of *la ama de casa*. The children attend private *liceos* or religious schools. These schools frequently offer bilingual education (for instance, *un colegio americano o alemán*) from kindergarten to *la preparatoria* (college prep schools), that lead after graduation to prestigious universities in Mexico or abroad. This prepares the children to later be part of the family's business empire.

As a strong institution, extended families can solve many problems and absorb hardships. Divorce is not one of them. Yet, as women's rights are slowly improving, so will intolerance for marital abuses and escapades; then divorce rates will increase and family traditions slowly erode.

Related Web link: mexconnect.com/mex_/ culxcomp.html—comparison of life between Mexico and the United States and Canada (E)

Being a Child in Mexico

No matter into which economic circumstances the child is born, whether it is lovingly placed into a hammock or tucked into a high-tech crib, the parents immediately start planning for *el bautizo*. Within a few days, the chosen *padrinos* (godparents), family, guests, and friends are summoned and the baby taken to church. The priest registers the vital statistics and everybody joins in a happy celebration of the new church member.

It is common that mothers from poor and low-income families carry their babies with them all the time. Tightly wrapped and held on their mothers' backs with a rebozo, they "rock" along through her endless daily chores. They are very visibly a part of public life. Experts agree that this particular physical closeness to the mother is why these babies hardly ever cry and seem to be so very content. In more affluent situations, parents shower their child with every toy and gadget available and nannies are employed to look after the baby. Fathers are marginally involved, until they finally notice that the child has grown into a young adult.

By the fifth birthday, the child's socioeconomic preconditioning is well at work. While a poor child might already be in the workforce selling *chicle* in the street, listlessly trying to find customers for a shoe shine, or helping with the chores around the house, the better off ones play with fancy toys, celebrate elaborate parties, are protected by an often large household staff, and are therefore slower to grow up.

In both cases, parental love and support is guaranteed, no matter what. When, eventually, class separation sends one group off to an overcrowded public school and the other to an isolated, private *liceo*, the middle class seems to be affected the most. There, parents usually want their children to get to a social level they themselves were unable to reach. In the end, however, they often have to find a compromise and supplement the available free education with afternoon or evening classes in computing, technology, or business math, to get them at least into a white-collar job.

Thirty-four percent of the total population in Mexico is under the age of fifteen, the age when girls and boys traditionally entered adulthood—a fact celebrated by *la quinceañera* for girls, when they are introduced to society as eligible for marriage. For boys there is nothing comparable, and in our times it doesn't have much relevance for either sex. Most of *los jovenes* (young people) are still in school and have not the least desire to marry and settle down. Only in the remote areas do some fifteen-year-old girls still face that reality. The rest of that segment of population still gets to play.

But before they reach this age, there are childhood games. The games of old have all but gone, except for baby games that are similar to those played everywhere: "This little piggy went to the market . . ." counts the fingers in Mexico as

Aquí está el niñito chiquitito,	Here is the cute little child,
aquí el señor de los anillos,	here the master of the rings,

mira el tonto	look at the crazy
y loco,	one,
y el que lama	and the one which
cazuelas,	cleans the bowl,
y el que mata	and the one that
pulgas.	kills the fleas.

Later on, girls play with dolls, either readily available Barbies or with handmade creations, accompanied by miniature setups of furniture, dishes, and decorations. Boys like action figures, often modeled after famous *luchadores* (wrestlers). Kids in the streets play with *canicas* (mar-

bles), *zancos* (stilts), and *títeres* (puppets); they fly *papalotes* (kites) or kick a soccer ball around. Often, imagination brings stones and sticks alive.

Technology and mass-produced toys have, of course, brought more changes. Computers are now an accessible commodity, either at home or in a growing number of cybercafés that allow access to video games and instant communication. Traditional toys from different regions are still made but are mostly sold as *artesanías* to tourists.

SOCIAL ISSUES
Survivors

Holding down a job would not be a problem for more than forty million hard-working Mexicans, but how to survive on a substandard *sueldo* (pay) on an hourly or daily basis is another question. It means relying heavily on the extended family and the stereotypical staple foods—tortillas and beans, as well as low-priced fruit and vegetables from the market or CONASUPO, a chain of government-subsidized stores. There is very little one can buy on what often amounts to less than US$2 per day. Even the official minimum wage (set differently by each state) rarely goes beyond a daily US$3.50.

To break out of that cycle of poverty is beyond most families. With everybody out and about during the waking hours, struggling for a peso here and there, very little time remains for long-term improvement of the economic situation through education and training, or simply to search out opportunities. Usually all effort and creativity is dedicated to eking out a living.

Examples of that kind of lifestyle include a cab driver who has to deliver US$30 to his *patrón*, the owner of the taxi, after six hours of hustling rides. What he makes beyond that amount he can keep. This is however calculated so tightly that on bad days he has to put in his own money—and he also must pay for the gas and minor repairs. Then there are the omnipresent street vendors of all ages, carriers moving back-breaking loads, and watchmen and security guards mostly working without any insurance, job security, and other benefits. A tour guide in the caves of Cacahuamilpa (near Taxco) has to support a family of four with a government check of 400 pesos (US$40) every other week if he is "lucky" enough to get in at least one two-hour tour a day. A lucky woman in La Unión, Gro., starts every morning at 6:00 A.M. in a small *tortillería* (tortilla "factory"), prepares the *nixtamal* (tortilla dough), feeds it into the machine, counts and stacks the fresh tortillas for ten hours, and gets paid 300 pesos (US$30) a week. Little wonder that many of these people, 40 percent of the Mexican population, jump at opportunities elsewhere, legal or illegal, at home or abroad. *El norte* (the United States) often offers the quickest solution.

If the overall economic situation seems to be rather hopeless for manual laborers, personal depression does not seem to be a problem. Frustration does, however, sometimes play out in family abuse, alcoholism, and, more often, men abandoning their families, situations that perpetuate the cycle of poverty as children have to help earn money, drop out of school, and, just like their parents, get caught in the daily struggle for survival.

Playing Ball: The Old Way of Tlachtli

Goals, touchdowns, home runs, slam dunks, fumbles, ties, time out . . . terminology we live with, sometimes breathe for. Team sports dominate conversations, and they are an easy common denominator.

It wasn't always so. Team sports, according to anthropologists, come from the ancient Americans, the Maya and the Aztecs. Tlachtli was the game played before the conquest. It was most likely a mixture of our basketball, tennis, soccer, or squash. There was a small vertical stone hoop, a double-T-shaped court slightly longer than a modern football field, and two teams with two to seven players on each side, playing with a rather hard rubber ball with elbows, hips, and knees and no other part of the body. The uniform included some cloth, padding, and a feathery headdress.

The game was not considered a pure spectator sport but rather a religious ritual. Scoring, by getting the ball through the small stone hoop mounted on the stone walls flanking the court, was nearly impossible. But points could be made by making the ball hit an opponent, or just by keeping it in possession.

The outcome of the game was hard to predict because of the unforeseen bounces of the ball off the many uneven surfaces. Therefore, tlachtli often served as a form of oracle, helping to make decisions. To enhance the power of the outcome, human sacrifice, with its ever-flowing blood, was necessary. It is not established if it was the losing team that had to die. Anthropological research suggests that for the greater glory, it was more likely that the winners had to be sacrificed.

Nowadays, tourists interested in reenactments of the game at some authentic ball courts may see for themselves what it was (probably) like. Especially in the Oaxaca region with sites like Monte Albán, Mitla, Dainzu, and others, it's worthwhile to check the calendar of events while touring the region.

Related Web links: ballgame.org—interactive website explains tlachtli (E); members.aol.com/cabrakan/ball.htm—explanation of the game, along with artifacts (E)

133

La lotería: ¡Pégale al gordo! (Hit the Big One!)

An impressive art-deco building on Mexico City's Reforma Avenue houses a national institution, La Lotería Nacional de Asistencia Pública, the national lottery for welfare. There, every Tuesday, Friday, and Sunday, a well-orchestrated group of twelve uniformed *niños gritones* (screaming children) perform the drawing and announce the winning numbers. On the major national holidays—Cinco de Mayo, September 15 (Independence Day), Christmas Day, and January 6 (Epiphany)—there are extra mega-drawings.

Lottery tickets can easily be obtained from strolling vendors or at newspaper stands. Each state also has a regional office. The tickets sold, however, address more than one need. While winning is still the goal, of course, the lottery also attempts to educate the public. National pride is disseminated by depicting icons of Mexican culture on the tickets, from sports to scientists, outstanding teachers, artists, writers, and social issues.

Gambling has been around in the Americas ever since the Spaniards unpacked their card games after the conquest. A royal decree of 1766 established a lottery in Peru for rebuilding funds after a devastating earthquake. Mexico followed in 1772 with a lottery for the benefit of the kingdom's poor and helpless. Nowadays la Corporación Iberoamericana de Loterias y Apuestas de Estado (CIBELAE, the Iberoamerican Corporation of Lotteries and Gambling) is an international organization that tries to set similar standards and maintain a charitable focus for the lotteries in Latin America and Spain.

Rumor has it that nobody ever wins anything. However, given the transparency of the drawing by those well-trained fifth graders it seems to be just that, a rumor. Also, in addition to the traditional listings in all major papers, the winning numbers can now be looked up on the lottery's official website: loterianacional.gob.mx.

For those who still doubt, there is the option of joining in another lottery, the very popular *juego de lotería*, a game of bingo played at local ferias (usually fairs in honor of a saint). Up to twenty players sit at tables around a stand, and in front of each is a board with sixteen pictures on it that correspond to cards in the singer's (announcer's) stack of fifty-four cards. The pictures are an odd collection of quaint drawings that include roosters, dandies, frogs, a brave apache, a boot, a skull, an anatomically correct heart, a star, a siren, and many more, the meaning of which has long been lost.

In the traditional way, the announcer "sings" little verses that refer to a drawing.

Verde, blanco	Green, white,
y colorado,	and red,
la bandera del	the soldier's flag.
soldado.	

If the flag is on your board you put a bean on it. Once you have four in a row you shout "*¡Lotería!*" and claim your prize—not the millions waiting at the national lottery when you hit the big one (*el gordo*), but something more realistic such as a stuffed animal or a shiny plastic (and empty!) wallet.

Home of the National Lottery, D.F.

Related Web link: lotenal.gob.mx—national lottery website (S)

La charreada: A Mexican Rodeo

A must for everyone visiting Mexico is to attend a *charreada* or *jaripeo* (a Mexican rodeo), a unique expression of Mexican culture. Excellent horsemanship, originating in Spain and adapted to the demands of the new world, has evolved into a sequence of fine-tuned rituals and performances within an arena generally called *el lienzo charro*, where the *suertes* (events) take place.

Within the space of a few hours the performances range from the most daring circus acts to flamboyant *escaramuzas*, the balletlike skirmishes of the *charras* (girls' riding team) who ride sidesaddle in flowing dresses, and then on to demonstrations of skills like *los piales* (roping horses' hind legs) and *el coleadero*, where the fast-riding *charro* grabs a bull's tail, wraps it around his boot, and makes the animal roll over sideways. And in *las rayadas*, precision and "horse sense" are essential: the *charro* approaches the center of the *lienzo* at full gallop, brings the horse to an abrupt halt, performs a few full and partial circles, and then backs the horse out of the arena.

Because of their splendid appearance, *charros* often are invited to enhance patriotic celebrations. Many towns in Mexico have a chapter of the Asociación Nacional de Charros that generally draws its members from the upper ranks of society. The first Spanish landowners quickly made money and rose socially by breeding horses and cattle. To show off, these nouveaux riches donned fancy suits lavishly adorned with silver whenever they had the opportunity, such as Sunday church services in town. After mass the men would linger and demonstrate their horsemanship and eventually compete with each other. In this respect the *charro mexicano* outdoes all other cowboys, from the gaucho of the Argentinean pampas to the buckaroo of the American West. His tradition today is still that of a Castilian *caballero* (gentleman).

Over the years the image of the *charro* has changed in accordance with shifting economic patterns. Today there are three distinct groups of Mexican *charros*: (a) the original "gentleman" *charros*, drawing members from those who can afford all the pomp and circumstance; (b) the "buckaroo" *charro*, a ranch hand, who takes care of livestock and training horses; and (c) the professional *charro*, the "rodeo cowboy," involved for the sport of it and competing in various disciplines based on the rules of the Asociación Nacional de Charros. The first group often employs the buckaroos and rodeo cowboys on their own *ranchos*.

Sunday noon, after mass, is still the best time to catch one of their performances—for example, at the Rancho del Charro in Chapultepec Park in Mexico City, or just ask for the closest *lienzo de charros* in almost any Mexican town.

Related Web link: nacionaldecharros.com— official website of the Asociación Nacional de Charros, including history, clothing, events, and lore (S)

Soccer and ¡Gooooooooo00000L!

Soccer has had a firm grip on the Mexican people ever since some Welsh immigrants brought the game to the mining town of Pachuca in the state of Hidalgo around 1900. Now, at any time and all over the nation, barefoot little boys are kicking a ball around, adolescents casually gather in pickup games on the village square, and, throughout local and regional leagues, young men play on teams all the way to the top of *la primera división* (first division). Here, eighteen teams follow a rigorous schedule through a winter and a summer season in four groups to compete for the championship. Among these teams are, for example, Los Pumas, a team from UNAM; Los Tusos (sheep) from Pachuca and Las Chivas (the goats) of the University of Guadalajara (who proudly claim to be *puro mexicano*, a team of 100 percent Mexican players); Los Diablos Rojos (the Red Devils) from Toluca; Los Camoteros (the candy makers) from Puebla; Los Toros (the bulls) of Nezahualcóyotl; Los Potros de Hierro (the iron colts) of América; and more.

Teams within the first division are distributed geographically in accordance with the distribution of the population. So there are six teams from Mexico City, and the colonial heartland is represented by other urban centers—three teams each from Guadalajara and Monterrey, and others from Puebla, León, Celeya, Pachuca, Morelia, and Toluca. If that seems to be geographically selective, a look at *la segunda división* will more than complete the national soccer map. Every year the two top teams of *la segunda* will ascend to the first division while the lowest two from *la primera* have to go down.

Soccer has not caught on with the indigenous population in the rural areas. Here only basketball is available because courts built alongside rural schools are an integral part of a basic infrastructure.

In Mexico, as in the rest of the world, soccer has become a multimillion dollar business that is heavily promoted by the media. It is at its best when Los Águilas and Las Chivas meet. Streets will be empty—just like Super Bowl Sunday in the United States. It's the time for *los superclásicos*. Every last seat in the stadium will be occupied—up to 100,000 spectators can be accommodated in the Estadio Guillermo Cañedo, formerly Estadio Azteca, in Mexico City.

Related Web link: femexfut.org.mx—official website of Federacón Mexicana de Fútbol, including profiles and histories of clubs (S)

Bullfighting: Art, Sport, or Sacrament?

Kinship between the Spanish and the indigenous cultures, and some thin blood relationship, might show at the popular celebration of the *corrida de toros* (the bullfight). Bloody and sacrificial ceremonies are actually part of most people's histories and traditions and have excited many cultures since the beginning of time. Rulers everywhere have known that *panem et circenses* (bread and circuses) will keep their citizens happy.

The bullfighting that the Spaniards brought the New World was a somewhat tamer version of the games inherited from the Romans, which had gladiators and savage beasts meeting in an arena. And the gladiatorial combat paled in comparison to the pre-Columbian ritual of human sacrifice in Mesoamerica.

The Catholic church was definitely opposed to gladiators, but it totally banned human sacrifice and destroyed most pagan sites throughout the new colonies. Bullfighting had already been a tradition long tolerated by the secular and clerical authorities in Spain, and now it took care of the entertainment needs of the population in the new territories. Bullfighting, although but a weak substitute for the Aztec sport of human sacrifice, quickly gained an important place in the postconquest traditions of Mexico, Colombia, and other Latin American countries—perhaps helped by the fact that the first corridas were indeed gory, bloody, and fatal for many an untrained torero and matador (actually "killer").

The first chronicled bullfight in Mexico took place on August 13, 1529, to honor the day of *San Hipólito* and the taking of Tenochtitlán, the Aztec capital, eight years previously. It was quite different from today's finely tuned performances of the world's best bullfighters. By 1790, when a grand *corrida* took place for Charles IV's coronation, bullfights in the New World had finally become the art form and spectacle they are today.

One of the best places in Mexico to witness a top performance is at the Plaza (de Toro) México in Mexico City, which seats about fifty thousand people. The main season, *la temporada formal*, is in the winter months, with fights usually on Sundays at 4:00 P.M. (always on time!). Many *corridas* can be watched on TV in your hotel room, but it's better to experience the live *ambiente* amongst the real aficionados.

In the United States, a trip to any Latino video store can get you a series of highlights of many a bullfight. You might even find a section advertising "incredible details and close-ups of a guaranteed number of matadors being maimed or killed in the arena." Could that be a reminder of the regular patrons' unconscious longing for their bloody past?

Related Web links: **bullfights.org**—news, schedules of major bullfights in Tijuana and Mexicali, access to "The Bullfight Store," and other links (E); **portaltaurino.com/mexico/mexico.htm**—rings, results, events, history (S); **gomexico.about.com/cs/culture/a/bullfights.htm**—essay on bullfighting (E)

Wrestling: *La lucha libre*

Followers of the American wrestling scene will be very familiar with the events in wrestling arenas. Even though wrestling was declared staged action some time ago by one of its organizations, the World Wrestling Federation (WWF), millions of fans still wholeheartedly buy into every aspect of it, applauding every intricate move of their favorites. This kind of sports entertainment, live or on TV, also may strike socially sensitive chords in the spectators: wrestling matches are often about the little guy getting back at "them."

In the United States, these magnificently choreographed events follow "plots" or "stories" and are supported by colorful and ominous names, such as "Hulk Hogan," "The Rock," or "The Undertaker." For Mexico, this holds partly true as well. However, *la lucha libre* has its very own, culturally significant characteristics. The wrestlers add symbolism by wearing masks that they never take off, except if they take on the challenge in a match of "mask against mask." Having been unmasked the loser has not only lost the match but also all prestige and honor (loss of face). The masks, along with the wrestler's name, can represent any archetypal force—death, fear, mythical gods, the devil, ancient heroes—but also characters taken from more recent mass media. So, El Espectro and Mr. Niebla (The Ghost and Mr. Fog) might wrestle with Tarzán and El Terremoto (Tarzan and the Earthquake), or Cien Caras (Hundred Faces) could take on El Rey del Infierno (the King of Hell). The legendary fighter El Santo, for example, always fought on the good side and he has become Mexico's John Wayne. But as these wrestling matches are based on the common Mexican culture, their stories are different. Ever-present social issues or specific government organizations often provide the plots.

That's exactly where we find "Super Barrio." This wrestler has actually stepped away from the arena and appears, somewhat like Superman, unannounced and unexpected at gatherings and public places to denounce aberrations in current society and take up the causes of the destitute, trying to instigate critical thinking, civil courage, and public action. Again, the mask helps him to be everybody and nobody at the same time.

Back in the Arena de México on Friday night, hundreds of aficionados line up outside to buy their tickets for their favorite seats. While waiting they have every opportunity to buy posters, masks, magazines, action figures, and costumes of their favorite *luchador* to build up the fervor that they then loudly and crudely release during the action in the ring. Spectators come from all walks of life, all ages and social levels, and both sexes, and are, at least for a while, on common ground.

Related Web links: cmll.com—Consejo Mundial de Lucha Libre (S); **triplea.com.mx**—Triple A wrestling (S)

Driving: *Poco a poco se va lejos*

When driving in Mexico there are a handful of different traffic signs, road conditions, and general driving attitudes to consider, including faster traffic flow. "Inspección" on a sign and an octagonal stop sign that says "ALTO" mean customs or military inspection; this is a time to be polite and cooperative. A big E (for *estacionamiento*, parking) in a red circle gives parking information, such as *una hora* (one hour), while NO with a crossed out E means no parking. "Ceda el paso" in an inverted triangle tells you to yield the right-of-way, and "No rebase" forbids passing another vehicle. A sign showing "] [" indicates a narrow (one-lane) bridge. "Circulación" with an arrow above is similar to "*Conserve su derecha* (Stay right)." "Vado" indicates a dip in the road, often a ford across a dry (or flowing) creek. The rest of the signs combine pictographs and Spanish cognates in a manner that makes them easily understood.

Because many roads are in disrepair with big potholes, suddenly discontinued or narrow lanes, unexpected and slow-moving vehicles drawn by livestock, horseback riders, and people or burros carrying bulky loads, it is advisable to drive with 100 percent concentration and *never* after dark.

To slow down cars in villages and towns there are *topes* (speed bumps) made of sidewalk-high asphalt bars or metal buttons across the road. Ninety-five percent of those are announced (e.g., "Topes 100 m"), but sometimes they are not. In the latter case "surprise" bumps might be extremely damaging to a car, probably a time to call *los*

ángeles verdes, green rescue trucks run by the official tourism office (SECTUR).

Remembering how, in general, life in Mexico is a daily struggle for most, to succeed in any endeavor becomes paramount. Translating this into driving attitudes helps understand traffic better. It is quite safe to drive in Mexico because everybody is very alert to the hustle and bustle of life everywhere along the roads. The flow of traffic might seem faster than in the United States, but rules are obeyed, more or less. In residential areas speed is limited to 40 kmh (25 mph), or 110 kmh (70 mph) on freeways. Driving in cities can seem scary because of multilane roads and roundabouts. Changing lanes or merging into nonstop traffic needs to happen quickly and with determination. The right-of-way has to be *taken*: *yielding* does not go with the prevailing—or macho—attitudes.

> Related Web link: americanrvrentals.com/
> mexicoterms.htm—Mexican road terms and
> signs (E)

Routes: Following a Theme

Some tourist destinations share a common theme. They are distributed along roads that tie them together based on pre-Columbian, colonial, or more modern history or folklore. These routes offer an excellent approach to absorb local ambiance and the Mexican culture in a bigger context, or to pursue recreational and educational pleasures tied to specific cultural background.

La Ruta de Las Flores is one such avenue. It highlights the lush tropical flora of the coastal plains throughout the wet and dry seasons. The ground is extremely fertile and the climate seems to make anything that's put in the ground grow, blossom, and bear fruit. *Bugambilias* (bougainvillea), *flamboyanes* (royal poinciana), jacaranda trees, and hundreds of different blooming vines and flowers overwhelm the traveler. This Road of the Flowers runs east to west from Veracruz to Orizaba and on toward Mexico City. It follows closely the first part of La Ruta de Cortés, which was the lifeline between the Spanish motherland and the new colonies in central Mexico. Along this road cities with evocative names like Córdoba and Puebla sprang up and the most intensive interactions between the Spaniards and *indigenas* took place. Another popular route is La Ruta Maya, which connects the major pyramids and archaeological sites (Palenque, Uxmal, Chichén Itzá, Tulum, Tikal, Copán) from the Yucatán Peninsula to Belize, Guatemala, and Honduras.

Various versions of La Ruta de Las Misiones can be retraced throughout Mexico, the U.S. Southwest, or any of the former Spanish possessions in the Americas.

In their systematic approach to expanding the empire, the Spaniards built small settlements within a single day's horseback ride along the new trade and communication routes. These outposts usually harbored a priest in charge of converting the local *indios*, some lay brothers to start a *rancho* for self-sufficiency, and a handful of soldiers to protect them all. Travelers could enjoy good food and a night of protected sleep.

The best preserved example for this kind of *ruta* is the Camino Real (the royal road) in Alta California (U.S. state of California) where one headstrong Franciscan brother, Junípero Serra, repeated that pattern twenty times en route from the mission of San Diego de Alcalá to Nuestra Señora de Dolores in San Francisco, Calif. His route built, of course, on the supply line of the mission trail on the Baja California peninsula where the Jesuits established a long chain of missions starting in Loreto in 1699. Most of those are in ruins or total disrepair since Benito Juárez' reform laws of 1858, which not only disestablished the church but also separated it completely from the state.

Related Web links: californiamissions.com—a virtual tour of Californian missions (E); **euronet .nl/~jeroen_k/mayan_route.htm**—personal page about traveling the Mayan route (E); **meso web.com/palenque**—archeological dig site (E)

Navigating the Metropolis

One-fifth of Mexico's population claims some of the living space in the area of the Valle de Anáhuac, the centrally located valley of Mexico City and the Distrito Federal. Exact numbers are not available, but twenty million people seems to be the conservative estimate nowadays. Few disagree with giving Mexico City the number one spot as the most populated metropolitan area on earth.

Of the many problems present, traffic, transportation, and the resulting pollution take high priority with the authorities. Driving private cars is, like everywhere else, the preferred choice of the *chilangos* (people from Mexico City). Restrictions based on license plate numbers and days of the week alleviate crowding and pollution somewhat—but make only a small dent. Motorcycles, mopeds, and bicycles prove most efficient for public transportation in the heavily congested downtown areas, but it is public transportation that bears the brunt as people movers.

Innumerable buses roar through the streets. While providing the most economic way of getting around, they also produce the most breathtaking black clouds of exhaust. Then there is *el metro* (the subway), ever expanding since the Olympic Games in 1968 but so congested at peak hours that people need to get packed into the cars. Especially avoid hubs such as Pino Suárez at those hours. Why not take a taxi? There are thousands of them. They are more expensive, of course, and will have to go with the (slow) flow of traffic: even the tiniest VW bug taxi won't go anywhere faster. And there are the *colectivos*, minivans with maximum interior space to accommodate maximum numbers of passengers, that cruise on fixed routes. They can be flagged down or caught at regular stops and cost much less than a taxi.

Now, what about the adventurous tourist who wants to explore the city? He or she would use all the above. For those with safety concerns, the front desk of the hotel will probably offer many options of organized bus tours. These are hassle free, but with the disadvantage of experiencing the country from a different, more distant point of view.

Related Web link: mexicocity.com.mx/mexcity.html—maps, history, and attractions (E, S)

El Camino Real: The Pan-American Highway I

La Panamericana is the longest continuous road system in the Americas. Officially, it starts at the southern U.S. border at four gateways: Nogales, Ariz., and Eagle Pass, El Paso, and Laredo, Tex., but it actually connects Prudhoe Bay in Alaska with Ushuaia at the southern tip of South America. The Pan-American highway has been an ongoing project since the 1920s and is still an issue for the Organization of American States (OAS), in particular for the Pan-American Highway Congress, which meets every four years.

Following La Panamericana from either one of the four border towns to Mexico City and then on to Guatemala will give those tourists particular to road trips an excellent overview of central Mexico, its people, culture, landscape, fauna, flora, and history.

From El Paso to Mexico City the travelers follow the route once known as the *camino real* of the expanding viceroyalty of New Spain. Splendid cities along the way offer all the modern amenities. A good example is Chihuahua at the center of rich cattle country with its colonial downtown and a marketplace where Tarahumara Indians from the nearby Copper Canyon offer their crafts, and German-speaking Mennonites sell what they produce on the lands the government granted them in 1921.

After a long haul through the sparsely populated deserts, Zacatecas with its exquisite colonial architecture offers a welcome break, stunning tourists with the display of its prosperous mining past. And then there is Querétaro, the city where the ill-advised emperor Maximilian was executed in 1867.

Before entering the sprawling Distrito Federal of Mexico City, it is extremely worthwhile to make two more stops. First at the archaeological site of Tula, ancient capital of the Toltec empire, with its 14-foot high warrior figures, and home of the Quetzalcoatl legend, the mythological god-king-snake-bird. Second, a feast for the eye, the monastery of Tepotzotlán. It is a splendid outburst of Mexican baroque, a fiesta of gilded shapes, colors, and movement exalting a uniquely Mexican spirituality—a superb example of the churrigueresque style (named after José Churriguera [1665–1723], a Spanish architect).

Related Web links: tourbymexico.com, mexconnect.com/mex_/areas.html—tourist sites (E); zacatecas.gob.mx—state site with tourist information (S)

South from Mexico City: The Pan-American Highway II

Escaping the confusion of Mexico City, La Panamericana heads for the towering volcanoes of Popocatépetl and Iztaccíhuatl, skirts them to the north, and descends into Puebla, another colonial jewel, home of *mole poblano* (a legendary regional sauce) and the Volkswagen plant, where the production of the new Beetle has recently created three thousand additional jobs.

On to Tehuacán where the nationally distributed Agua Tehuacán originates, and Oaxaca, yet another irresistible tourist attraction, with the ruins of Monte Albán, Mitla, and Dainzu; the biggest tree of the Americas, *el árbol del Tule*, a 2,000-year-old cypress with a circumference of 58 m (190 ft); mescal distilleries; and a baffling variety of *artesanías* in nearby villages.

At Juchitán the highway reaches the Isthmus of Tehuantepec—once thought of as an alternative site for the Panama Canal—then climbs up into the highlands of Chiapas leading to the capital of the state, the surprisingly modern and bustling Tuxtla Gutiérrez. Although the close-by Sumidero Canyon attracts many visitors, everybody around Tuxtla seems to be just passing through to San Cristóbal de las Casas. There, the traveler can marvel at the stoic Tzotzils, Tzeltals, and Chamulas who for centuries of isolation have kept their ancient ways. Events in the last fifty years, however, have started to narrow the gap. Intrusive tourism has alerted them to an outside world, making them realize how miserably their government had failed them. Then in 1994 came Subcoman-

dante Marcos of the Ejercito Zapatista para la Liberación Nacional (EXLN), whose strategical calls drew the attention of the world to this forgotten region of Mexico. Playing a global deck of cards, Marcos skillfully exploited the electronic revolution to spread everywhere the word of the Zapatista ideology, demanding land redistribution and indigenous self-determination.

But La Panamericana goes on, to Comitán and Ciudad Cuautemoc at the Guatemalan border, El Salvador, Honduras, . . . and eventually Tierra del Fuego in Argentina.

Related Web links: lonelyplanet.com/theme/roadtrips/road_panamerican.htm—background information on the Pan-American highway; vanagon.com/journeys/caravana/index.html—follow an actual trip along the Pan-American highway

La Plaza Garibaldi: Mexico in Miniature

Plaza Garibaldi, in the heart of the capital, offers a great variety of what some tourists expect to see in Mexico. The good times here always include tequila accompanied by an array of tasty *antojitos* (hors d'oeuvres) and enhanced by music of many regions and the general crowded *ambiente*—smells and excitement—of feria and fiesta that permeates the air.

Just a few blocks north of Alameda Park, Plaza Garibaldi exemplifies the whole country in terms of *ambiente turístico*. It is a tourist trap for sure, but it offers a great learning experience (a fork in the road to choose between immersion and observation). Above all, it is a grand confusion of what Mexico stereotypically represents to the outside world. The plaza is surrounded by restaurants, bars, *cantinas*, stands, and booths with street vendors catering to every visitor's wish. In La Tenampa, a popular restaurant/bar, tequila is served straight up with *sal y limón* (salt and lime), with sangrita, or (as many gringos like it) in a frothy margarita. A spicy *ceviche* (a fish cocktail) might demand an ice-cold *cerveza* from one of the many good domestic breweries.

Sooner or later, strolling mariachis will come by the table and offer some kind of entertainment. Ask for any typical song such as "El rey," "Guadalajara," "Ojos negros," "El jinete," or "El caballo blanco," and by no means exclude the most popular gringo choices of "El rancho grande," "Cielito lindo," or "Malagueña salerosa." The musicians expect to be paid.

Before returning to the Plaza outside, feeling good, locals and visitors alike tuck away their wallet, passport, etc., in a safe place. It is usually very crowded, and vendors, panhandlers, children selling *chicle*, and *ladrones* (pickpockets) are waiting. Various mariachi bands play simultaneously—here for a shyly smiling Mexican couple, there for a rowdy group of locals or a busload of tourists. Somewhere, and less conspicuously, a three-man *conjunto jarocho* (a trio from Veracruz) is probably singing the ever popular "La bamba," accompanied by the harp, guitar, and a five-stringed *jarana*.

And for a real macho it is essential to impress his entourage by holding on to the two poles of an electrostatic machine while, for a few pesos, the smiling salesman slowly increases the charge—until he is begged to stop.

Related Web link: photoatlas.com/pics01/ pictures_of_mexico_05.html—scene of Plaza Garibaldi (E)

Border Crossings: The Expatriates

Many Mexican commuters cross over the border to the north, matter-of-factly, on their daily trip to work. At the same time, a great number of undocumented immigrants scramble, run, and, in increasing numbers, die to be *en el norte*, the land of unconfined opportunities. Simultaneously an undefined but smaller number of American citizens goes exactly the other way, to look for opportunities in their international careers or to stretch their retirement income into favorable peso expenses. They are called *los expatriados* (expatriates), Americans living abroad anywhere in the world, sometimes called the fifty-first state. They are an extremely fluid group, and very elusive to statistical data gatherers. Estimates of how many U.S. citizens actually live in Mexico vary widely and wildly.

First comes the hurdle of labeling. Are they permanent or temporary residents? Do they own real estate in Mexico? Do they rent? Are they Mexican-Americans returned with U.S. citizenship? Are they married to a Mexican citizen? Are they on a temporary stay, expats living in Mexico with U.S. income, or expats residing in Mexico and frequently commuting to their other home in the United States? Second, holding a valid U.S. passport allows a citizen to go anywhere, with neither side of the border keeping specific and coordinated track of the paper slips left behind in the immigration booth on entering Mexico.

There has been considerable pressure since 9/11 to control the border better. Both sides have been working on improvements. Mexico has recently announced plans to issue an identification card for all foreigners planning to live in Mexico for extended periods.

It is a fact that Mexico hosts more expatriate Americans than any other country, but statistics vary widely. According to the American embassy in Mexico City, fewer than 150,000 Americans live in Mexico "officially." Academic research, unofficially, claims that up to 1.5 million U.S. citizens make their home in Mexico.

Ironically, the U.S. partisan machinery might provide the most motivated and accurate statistical assessment of all. In recent U.S. elections, about two million people were targeted by mail, rallies, and speakers who made their rounds to address the expats of both major U.S. parties as potential absentee voters. In the numbers game, this might again average down to a more realistic 1.5 million Americans residing in Mexico, as academic research suggests.

How many Americans really live south of the border may be clouded for a while in elusive statistics. It is much easier to find out *where* they live.

The areas Americans flock to generally combine a pleasant climate with a sound infrastructure and a safe environment. These are conditions that especially the older expatriates hope to find. There is the prime example of the well-tended and often gated communities in Guadalajara and south to the beautiful setting of Chapala Lake. There, the town of Ajijic has probably the greatest number of U.S. retirees, followed perhaps by the picturesque San Miguel de Allende in the state of Guanajuato and Morelia, the capital of the state of Michoacán. The Baja peninsula offers above all proximity to the United States, easy access, and a population that has accommodated American travelers and adventurers for generations. It is dotted with thousands of time-share condominiums and outright American subdivisions, from Rosarito Beach on the Pacific or San Felipe on the Sea of Cortés all the way to Los Cabos. This includes a growing American colony in the pleasant, all-Mexican town of La Paz.

Mexico City has the biggest overall colony of Americans. In spite of continuous State Department warnings, thousands of expats live there, doing business, working with the U.S. embassy, teaching, or enjoying their retirement in a culturally stimulating metropolitan area.

Most Americans, once they have spent some time in Mexico, tend to fall in love with the kindness of the people and life in the slow lane. For those who get "caught," there are places that fit all comfort levels. Americans of every age and background can find what they are looking for. The adventurous look for the marginal geographic or socioeconomic areas and radically immerse themselves in the new culture, while others settle in communities with kindred spirits who enjoy maintaining their own culture and language while engaging in American-style community involvement.

Expats are often overlooked in the heated discussion of border crossings. While never legally challenged, their southward movement is as motivated by the desire for a higher quality of life as it is for the many Mexicans who cross the border the opposite way.

The expats' top twenty places

Coastal	Inland
Puerto Vallarta	Guadalajara/Ajijic/Lago Chapala
Zihuatanejo	San Miguel de Allende
Acapulco	Cuernavaca
San Carlos Bay	Mexico City
San Blas	Morelia
Cancún	Oaxaca
Los Cabos	Monterrey
La Paz	Mérida
Manzanillo	Puebla
Huatulco	San Cristóbal de las Casas

Related Web links: solutionsabroad.com/a_citiesmexico.asp—city profiles and services for expatriates (E, S); mexperience.com/liveandwork/living_in_mexico.htm—comprehensive look at living in Mexico (E)

Driving *into* Mexico: Border Protocol

Rumor has it that driving in Mexico is dangerous. Nevertheless, a great number of tourists choose to do just that. And they usually find out that, while it is definitely different, it's not that dangerous at all but offers a close-up look at Mexico on the street level. It is a unique chance to actually "do as the Mexicans do," which is hard to accomplish otherwise. A road trip becomes an instant immersion into popular culture.

To enter Mexico in a private vehicle does not have to be a bureaucratic nightmare that starts with red tape at the border, only to continue with unfamiliar driving behaviors enforced by corrupt cops, and/or ends with a highway robbery. Being alert in any of the three cases can easily steer you away from many troubles.

First comes the necessary *papeleo* (red tape)

1. Appropriate immigration forms: a tourist card (obtained at Mexican consulates) besides a valid passport (or just a birth certificate for U.S. citizens). It's important to keep the tourist card until leaving the country; they will ask for it.
2. A valid vehicle registration certificate (certifying legal ownership). Note: if the vehicle is registered in more than one name, the co-owner not present at the time of border crossing has to send along a notarized permission.
3. A rental/leasing contract in the name of the person driving the (rental) car.
4. A valid driver's license (international/non-Mexican). U.S. licenses are also valid in Mexico.
5. A credit card (Mastercard, Visa, American Express, Diner's Club, and others), again in the name of the owner of the vehicle. Without a credit card a bond has to be posted or a cash deposit of US$500–$20,000 paid, depending on the make and the year of vehicle.

Patience in dealing with border formalities is a good introduction to the pace it takes to interact with "official" Mexico. It is part of the leisurely approach to life in general. Time here is not money; it simply is!

With the breaking of the long-time political power of the PRI in 2000 a new breeze is airing out the old and corrupt bureaucratic system. One might, however, still run into officials, at the border or elsewhere, who ask for payments without giving a receipt or skillfully employ delay tactics in order to elicit *una mordida*.

How the tourist should react is up to his/her language skills. Often it helps to ask for *el jefe/gerente* (boss/manager) of the premises and explain the situation *with patience*!

Related Web link: mexconnect.com/mex_/ driving.html—regulations and information for drivers (E)

Los Colores

After having spent most of his adulthood working and living in Mexico, an expatriate contemplated moving back to where he came from, to "somewhere quieter," he said, where the "colors were not so shrill and piercing." By creating this *sinestesia* (mixed media image) he came up with a perfect metaphor for life in Mexico. It is never silent to any of the senses—they are all constantly alert.

In the olden days, a simple walk down the street in the early morning brought them all together. The sun feels good on the skin, lighting up the bold juxtapositions of bright, wildly contrasting colors on houses, doors, shutters, vendors' carts, the sky, and the clear white of traditional clothes of the indigenous people; a waft of the warm, nutritious smell from the *tortillería* that had just started cranking out piles of fresh tortillas, mixed with the light transparent smoke drifting through the trees. *Las urracas* (magpies) perform their wake-up concert in the spectacular *flamboyanes* around the zocalo, a good time to taste a fresh *café de olla*, which la señora on the corner sold out of the front door of her house next to the baker's basket full of *pan dulce*. . . .

Modern ways have not yet destroyed these idyllic scenes outside the metropolitan areas. Technological progress may have increased the noise and smog, sped up the pace of life, and changed eating habits, but it never has quite paled the extensive palette of colors. Stark contrasts—black and white extremes—created by economy and politics could not yet suffocate the colorful outbursts of Mexican identity. Fire-

works, ceremonies, music and dances, religious traditions, colorful splendor, and above all, *la fiesta*. Octavio Paz, Nobel laureate, explains in his masterwork, *El laberinto de la soledad*, "through fiesta, the Mexican opens himself up to the world, mixes and mingles with his own people and values which, in turn, impart meaning to his own religious and social being." *Fiesta* means explosion and escape; and it is a big part of the Mexicans' identity and helps them transcend all limitations.

And there are always opportunities to "party." If it isn't Christmas and the nine preceding days of posadas, then it's fiesta, family celebrations of birthdays, anniversaries, baptisms, and, for sure, the ferias in honor of the patron saints of every big and little church in the country. That way, joyful exuberance can do what neither pragmatic black-and-white thinking nor logic can accomplish: closing the gap between the extremes.

The Zapatista movement (EZLN) in the southern state of Chiapas perfectly demonstrates that irreverence to reality, the blurring of sharply drawn lines, even in serious military confrontations. Their Subcomandante Insurgente Marcos called the whole world's attention by using the Internet to paralyze further government action, extensively quoting Dante's *Inferno* and later promoted his case further by publishing a bilingual children's book in the United States, initially with the help of the National Endowment for the Arts (help that was later withdrawn), fittingly called *La historia de los colores* (*The Story of Colors*), a folktale from the jungles of Chiapas. **149**

Well, our expatriate eventually decided, after further contemplation, not to take any extreme action and to stay in the country to which he had become so attached. However, he will find a more serene place out in the Mexican countryside where the cacophony of colors will be more subdued. With that easy decision he also avoids bringing the extremes back into a disturbing focus. And one day he will, like most Mexicans, wholeheartedly agree, singing along with teary eyes to that old favorite tune written by Chucho Monge, *México lindo y querido*.

This song belongs to the immediate repertoire of all Mexican people, as well as the major Mexican tenors, from Jorge Negrete and Vicente Fernandez to today's Placido Domingo. It is an all-time Mariachi favorite, sung among many others, *con ganas*, by the great José Alfredo Jiménez. It exalts Mexico, every shade of its many colors, its music, and the land and the earth where every good Mexican wants to find his final rest.

Related Web link: elmariachi.com/songs/ mexico_lindo.asp—lyrics to the song *México lindo y querido* (E, S)

QUIZLINK ANSWERS

Artesanías
1. c, 2. b, 3. b, 4. a

El Norte
5. b, 6. b, 7. c, 8. b, 9. c, 10. b, 11. c

Consumerism
12. b, 13. a, c, b, 14. a, 15. c, 16. a, 17. b, 18. c

Economy
19. c, 20. c, 21. b, 22. b, 23. c

Education
24. b, 25. a, 26. c

Fiestas
27. b, 28. a, 29. b, 30. a, 31. b, 32. c, 33. a

Fine Arts and Music
34. a, 35. c, 36. c, 37. a, 38. b, 39. a, 40. b, 41. c

Folklore
42. a, 43. b, 44. a, 45. b, 46. a

Food
47. c, 48. a, 49. b, 50. b, 51. c, 52. b,a,c, 53. c

Government
54. c, 55. a, 56. b

History
57. b, 58. c, 59. c, 60. b, 61. c, 62. b, 63. c

Home and Family
64. c, 65. b, 66. a, 67. b, 68. b

The Land
69. a, 70. c, 71. a, 72. a, 73. b, 74. a

Language
75. c, 76. c, 77. b, 78. a, 79. c, 80. c, 81. b

Media
82. c, 83. a, 84. a

National Icons
85. b, 86. b, 87. b, 88. c

Religion
89. c, 90. c, 91. b

Social Issues
92. b, 93. c, 94. a, 95. c, 96. b, 97. a

Sports and Entertainment
98. b, 99. b, 100. a, 101. b, 102. b, 103. a

Tourism
104. a, 105. c, 106. a, 107. a, 108. a, 109. c, 110. b, 111. c

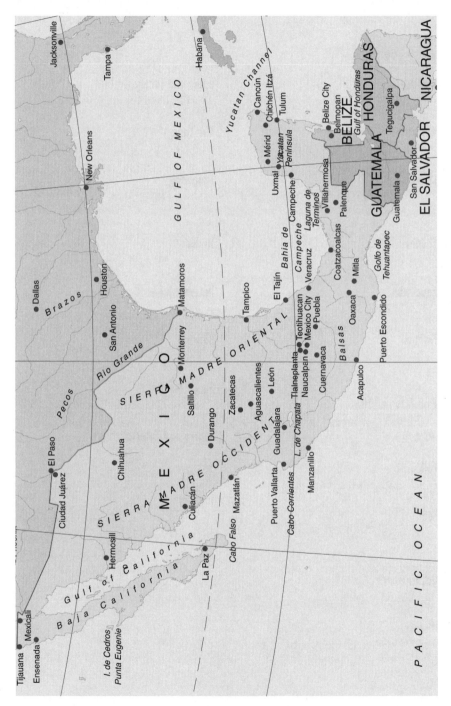

153

INDEX

INDEX

INDEX

INDEX

INDEX